THE COMPLETE BOOK OF ORIGAMI

Step-by-Step Instructions in Over 1000 Diagrams

37 ORIGINAL MODELS

Robert J. Lang

Photography by Robin Macey

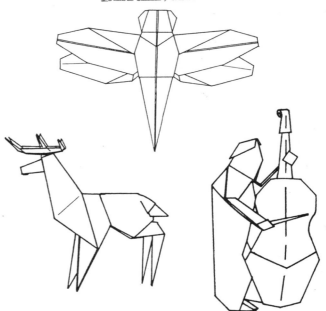

DOVER PUBLICATIONS, INC.
NEW YORK

To
Jim
Carolyn
Greg
Marla
and always,
Diane

Copyright © 1988 by Robert J. Lang.

All rights reserved under Pan American and International Copyright Conventions.

Published in Canada by General Publishing Company, Ltd., 30 Lesmill Road, Don Mills, Toronto, Ontario.

Published in the United Kingdom by Constable and Company, Ltd., 10 Orange Street, London WC2H 7EG.

The Complete Book of Origami: Step-by-Step Instructions in Over 1000 Diagrams / 37 Original Models is a new work, first published by Dover Publications, Inc., in 1988.

Manufactured in the United States of America
Dover Publications, Inc., 31 East 2nd Street, Mineola, N.Y. 11501

Library of Congress Cataloging-in-Publication Data

Lang, Robert J.
    The complete book of origami : step-by-step instructions in over 1000 diagrams / Robert J. Lang.
        p.   cm.
    Bibliography: p.
    ISBN 0-486-25837-8 (pbk.)
    1. Origami.   I. Title.
TT870.L26   1988
736'.982—dc19
                                                                    88-23260
                                                                    CIP

Foreword

Since the 1950s, origami has been making a return. Several American folders now rank among the world's leading creators of original figures. Why should this be so? I believe that it is because of a coincidence; the confluence of two different ideas of beauty.

Origami appeals to the Japanese sense of understatement. Just as a three-line haiku evokes a setting or a season, a few brush strokes suggest an entire bamboo plant. An art of suggestion, origami implies without announcing outright.

Origami is, likewise, an art of economy. A few simple creases evoke an animal; modify the sequence slightly, and an entirely new beast appears. To the Japanese sensibility, the success of a completed origami model depends on the creator's eye for form, structure and proportion. Does it capture the creature's true form, the placement of its head and limbs, the shape of its shoulders and hips? Does it suggest the animal's motion, its stride, glide or gallop? And finally, is the paper figure a mere likeness of the original, or does it delve deeper, into its essential character?

In America, origami was taken up not by artists but by scientists, engineers and architects. Enter, in the 1950s, a new set of aesthetic standards, the values of the geometer. The mathematician's idea of beauty draws its inspiration from an ideal world, a world of regularity, symmetry and order. Beauty is identified by simplicity and economy: Euclid's axioms, the Pythagorean theorem, harmonic motion. Freed from the constraints of the physical world, mathematics partakes of the world of dreams. Mathematical beauty is a geometric solid floating in space, gravity defied. It is the simplicity of $e^{i\pi} = -1$, the elegance of the shortest mathematical proof.

To the mathematician, the beauty of origami is its simple geometry. Latent in every piece of paper are undisclosed geometric patterns, combinations of angles and ratios that permit the paper to assume interesting and symmetric shapes. The mathematician asks: Does this model make the greatest use of the existing geometry? Is the folding procedure elegant and pristine, with crisp lines, compact folds, simple and regular proportions? Is there no wasted paper, awkward thickness or arbitrary fold? Is utility served in each step?

Robert Lang's origami models exemplify both Japanese and American standards of beauty. They are anatomically accurate (an American demand, not a Japanese one) yet they suggest more than they show. Ingeniously crafted, like miniature machines, they reveal a protean inventiveness. (His exploration of action folds, for example, has no parallel.) While his folding techniques are often unexpected, they are never arbitrary, and on occasion they reveal their logic only after the entire figure has been completed.

In common with creative artists of any epoch, Lang seizes upon simple, timeless forms and manipulates them so that they emerge as never before. To fold his origami models is to experience the beauty shared by the mathematician and the Japanese brush painter.

—Peter Engel

Acknowledgments

This book arose from conversations in 1983 with Alice Gray and Lillian Oppenheimer of the Origami Center of America. Their advice was invaluable, and I thank them for it. John Montroll gave me several helpful suggestions on the drawings, Stephen Weiss gave me suggestions on origami symbols, and Peter Engel offered suggestions on both. Louise Cooper was a constant source of encouragement when I was juggling book drawings and West Coast Origami Guild activities. Robin Macey showed great skill and patience in shooting and reshooting the photographs. I am tremendously indebted to my wife, Diane, for her tireless editing, proofreading, rereading and recommendations on layout. To all of the above, I give my heartfelt thanks.

The Author

Robert J. Lang began at the age of six folding origami from a book not unlike this one. In the twenty-odd years since, he has invented over 200 original figures and exhibited his models worldwide, including origami conventions in New York and London. He has written a regular column on current topics in the art for the journal "British Origami" since 1985, and has written several other articles on the subject for various journals, newspapers and an encyclopedia. A physicist by trade, he lives in Altadena, California, where he is on the research staff of the Jet Propulsion Laboratory. He is now working on his second origami book in collaboration with Stephen Weiss.

PHOTO: BOB PAZ

Table of Contents

History

Origami is the art of folding uncut sheets of paper into decorative objects such as birds or animals. The word for this ancient Japanese art comes from *ori-*, meaning "folded," and *-kami*, meaning "paper." Almost any subject is suitable for an origami model, despite the stringent limitation of using an uncut sheet, and origami models come in all sizes and degrees of complexity. Origami artists have made birds 1/64th of an inch long, and life-size elephants three yards high. The number of creases in a model can range from just a few to literally hundreds. The detail in complex folds can be astounding, for the artists of the modern era have carried origami to unprecedented heights of realism and complexity. While a simple bird can take less than a minute to make, it is not uncommon for an advanced folder to take two to three hours on a complicated insect. Most of the advances in origami have come within the past fifty years, but it is an old art; its origins go back to the invention of paper itself.

The art of papermaking was developed in China, and from there it traveled to the rest of the world. Buddhist monks carried paper to Japan in the 6th century A.D., and the first Japanese origami folds date from that period. At first, paper was a scarce commodity, and its use was limited to ceremonial occasions. The folds developed for these occasions were simple. They were stylized representations of animals, costumed people, or ceremonial designs, and although the modern ethic forbids it, the traditional folds frequently used cuts in the paper. The designs were passed down through the generations from mother to daughter. There were few written records of origami designs, and so the only folds that lasted were simple ones. Nevertheless, many of the traditional folds have an enduring beauty, and their simplicity is appealing. In more recent times, folding has appeared in the Western world. The Spanish, too, have a long tradition of paperfolding, although not as old as that of Japan. Simple folds tend to be reinvented over and over; thus, many of the same folds have come out of both the East and the West. Even America has a tradition of paperfolding; rare is the schoolchild who has never folded a hat, boat, plane or the ubiquitous fortune-teller or "cootie-catcher."

Paper is essential in printing, and it was perhaps inevitable that someone would combine printing and folding to produce the printed origami instruction. No one knows exactly when this happy marriage first occurred; however, some of the oldest existing directions are contained in the *Sembazuru Orikata*, or *Folding of 1000 Cranes*, printed in Japan in 1797.* In the West, early books include *Fun with Paperfolding* by Murray and Rigney (1928, reprinted by Dover Publications) and *Houdini's Paper Magic*.** The art received a

---

*The crane is a traditional Japanese symbol of good luck, and folding a thousand of them is supposed to grant the folder one wish. The tradition became common knowledge after World War II, when Sadako Sasaki, a young Japanese girl, contracted leukemia from the effects of the Hiroshima atomic blast. She made her wish to get well, and set out to fold 1000 cranes, but died 365 cranes short of her goal. Her classmates folded the rest (which were buried with her). Her story subsequently fired the world's emotions. Since then, the origami crane has become a symbol of international peace.

**Origami seems to hold a particular attraction for magicians—an astounding number of paperfolders are professional or amateur magicians. The late president of the British Origami Society, Robert Harbin, was a world-famous conjuror. He was also probably responsible for attracting many magicians to origami by his authorship of an origami book with the somewhat misleading title *Paper Magic*.

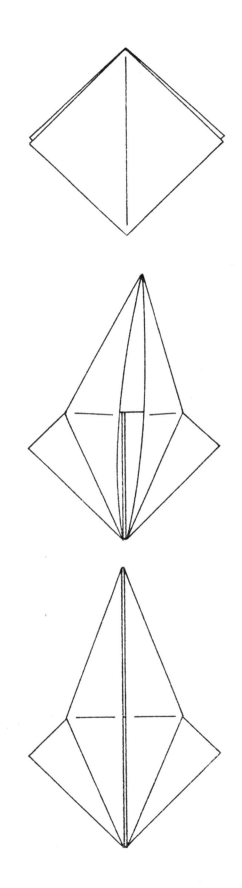

tremendous boost in the 1950s and 60s from the invention of a systematic code of dots, dashes and arrows by the Japanese folder Akira Yoshizawa, who is now regarded as the world's greatest paper-folder. This code was adopted by the western authors Harbin and Randlett in the early 1960s, and with minor alterations, has been used in nearly all origami books since. It is possibly the most important contribution to the art yet (save paper, of course). It has allowed the worldwide communication of folds and techniques in a language common to all; it is so universal that folders routinely purchase foreign origami books and work the folds from the diagrams alone. With minor variations, the code has been the standard for the past quarter-century, and it is the code used in this book.

The 1960s saw a flurry of activity in the Western folding world; they also saw the establishment of two origami societies. The Friends of the Origami Center of America and the British Origami Society supply books, paper, and tools, and publish newsletters containing items of interest to folders. Both the Friends and the BOS are international origami organizations with memberships that extend around the world.

The activity of the 1960s has inspired a generation of folders, and the art has branched out into many new directions. The flat, two-dimensional folds of yesterday have been joined by "modular" folds, in which many identical folds are assembled into a single multi-faceted shape.* There is a (perhaps reactionary) movement toward folding the subjects of modular folds—multipointed stars—from single sheets. There is interest in three-dimensional folds and folds that combine several subjects into a single fold—even action figures, figures that move when tugged. The shape of the paper is no longer restricted to the traditional square, but may be rectangular or otherwise polygonal. (There is, however, general agreement that shapes with corner angles greater than 180 degrees, for example, stars, are forbidden.) Many folds are made from dollar bills. Origami has found its way into the scientific disciplines in devious ways—an engineer patented a new type of airfoil he discovered while folding a paper airplane,** and the "reverse fold" has been shown to be useful in simulating optical systems.†

The folds in this book cover a broad range of complexity and difficulty, which are not necessarily the same thing. My goal has been to provide introductory material for the novice as well as challenge for the expert. The beginner should work through the models *in order*, as each of the introductory folds introduces one or two key procedures. Subsequent models build upon the results of previous models, so if you skip a model in the introductory sections, it will eventually catch up to you. The designs also get harder as you work through the chapters. I have included separate sections on three-dimensional and action folds that are still more advanced.

As you work through a fold, you should look at each step and *read the accompanying text*. I cannot emphasize this point enough. I mentioned earlier that many folders work from diagrams only; that technique will not work with this book. Particularly in the later models, the individual steps are complex. Often, there are many layers in a single flap, and I can't draw them all (due to limitations of pen width and space). The text accompanying the drawing will often provide

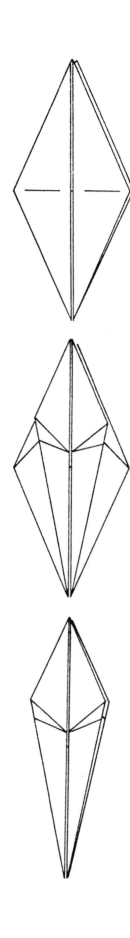

---

*However, there are those (myself included) who question the consistency of an ethic that allows the use of multiple sheets of paper but allows no cuts if you use only a single sheet. The cuts/no cuts controversy is primarily a Western issue. In Japan (where, after all, the art was invented) there are many artists who allow any cuts that don't remove paper (e.g., slits), and Yoshizawa, recognized as the world's greatest living folder, has many models that are made from two sheets of paper.

**R. Kline and F. Fogelman, *The Ultimate Paper Airplane*, Simon & Schuster, 1986.

†J. H. Myer, "Optigami—a tool for optical systems design," *Applied Optics*, vol. 8, no. 2, p. 260 (1969).

essential information for the completion of that step. So, I repeat: look at a step, read the text, and then look ahead at the next step to see what the result should look like; then fold the paper in the indicated manner. It is important to make the creases as precise as possible. Corner folds should run all the way to a point. Angle bisectors should precisely bisect the angle. With care and perseverance you should produce some beautiful sculptures and, I hope, derive the pleasure and satisfaction that I derive from this fascinating art.

Tools and Materials

In theory, at least, the only tools you need for origami are your hands, and the only material, a sheet of paper. In practice, there are a few more tools that may simplify matters. For cutting paper, a pair of scissors or an X-acto knife would be useful (I prefer the latter); also, you will need a ruler or straightedge and a cutting board if you are using a knife. In complex folds, a pair of needle-nosed tweezers will come in handy. In some of the complicated insects, they are a must. Many folders use a "folding bone" to burnish creases, but any hard, smooth object—a spoon, a wooden ruler or your thumbnail—will work just as well.

Many types of paper are suitable for origami. Traditional origami paper is precut to squares, brightly colored on one side (an essential feature for folds that exploit the two different colors), and is available from many craft sources. On the other hand, it is somewhat expensive, the texture and foldability varies with the manufacturer, sometimes it is not cut very exactly, and it is unavailable in the more esoteric shapes such as triangles or oddly proportioned rectangles. For those models, you will have to cut your own paper, so you might as well buy what's cheap. For general practice and experimentation, you can buy a ream (500 sheets) of regular bond paper for a few dollars; it will last you forever. Other possibilities include wrapping paper (especially the foil-backed kind) and art papers. You should keep an eye out for unusual patterns or textures in paper. Some craft stores sell a fuzzy, light cardboard that makes wonderful soft animals.

As a fold becomes more complex, the tensile properties of the paper assume greater importance. For example, the first fold in this book, the White-faced Mouse, could be folded out of almost anything—tissue, newspaper, sheet metal, you name it. A more complicated fold (such as the Deer) requires a thin, crisp paper for best results. The Cicada is just about impossible to fold from a thick or weak paper. The considerations when choosing a paper are thickness, strength, ability to hold a crease, crispness (how well flat surfaces support themselves) and forgiveness (how much a crease damages the paper). These qualities, however, cover conflicting objectives. A crisp paper gives clean lines to a model but does not lend itself to subtle shaping and gentle curves. Thick paper takes creases better than thin paper, but complicated models, which have many layers of paper in them, will burst at the seams if made from thick paper. Foil-backed paper (wrapping paper) has become very popular for complex folds. It holds creases extremely well, it has moderate tensile strength, and it can be readily shaped. Unfortunately, it has abominable forgiveness—the slightest wrinkle leaves a permanent mark on the surface, and the paper weakens drastically after it has been creased a few times. The shiny, metallic surface is not particularly appealing in many folds, but that problem can be circumvented by folding the metallic side toward the inside of a model. Nevertheless, every model in this book can be folded from foil paper, so you might want to invest in some. It is often sold in stationery stores with wrapping paper. Many art stores also carry it in large single sheets, and you can usually get the thinnest paper there.

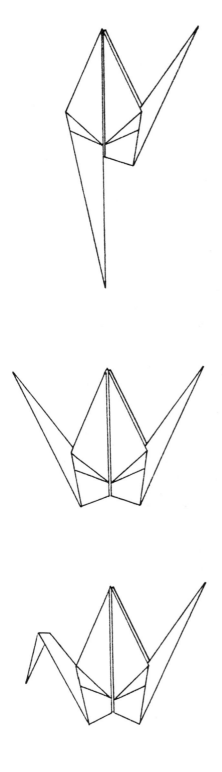

Still, only the last few folds in the book require any paper other than ordinary bond. My personal favorite for all-purpose folding is nine-pound manifold, also called "second sheet." It's the kind of paper used in multicarbon forms, and is available from office supply stores in a variety of colors, mostly drab pastels. It is the same color on both sides, so you can't use it for models that use both sides of the paper to achieve two different colors (for example, the White-faced Mouse). It is very inexpensive, and quite versatile.

When you cut your own paper, you should be absolutely certain to cut it to the exact proportions you need. Corners should be absolutely square for rectangles, sixty degrees for equilateral triangles, etc. (Don't count on any of the corners of a rectangle you have bought to be square; paper manufacturers vary greatly.) Origami is an art in which small errors at the beginning are amplified throughout the course of a fold. Starting with a trapezoid instead of a square is almost guaranteed to end unsatisfactorily.

My folds often use oddly proportioned rectangles. I have adopted the convention of specifying a rectangle as "1:x," where "x" is the length of the long side of the rectangle. To convert this to real dimensions, multiply "x" by the desired short side of the rectangle. For example, suppose the rectangle were specified as "1:2.138," and you wanted the short side of the rectangle to be 15 cm long. You would multiply 2.138 by 15 cm (preferably on a calculator) to get 32.07 cm; the resulting rectangle should be 15 cm by 32.07 cm. Some of the more common sizes of rectangle are 1:1 (a square), 1:1.414 (European letter paper, also called A4), 1:1.294 (American letter paper, or 8½ by 11 inches) and 1:2.360 (a dollar bill).

THE TRADITIONAL
JAPANESE CRANE

As with most specialized activities, origami has its own language of words and symbols, each with a specific meaning. The symbols are pretty much standardized, at least for basic sequences. There is some variation in symbols for the more complicated sequences. A list of the symbols and terminology precedes the folding instructions. They are introduced one or two at a time in this first section of folds.

When you make a single fold in a sheet of paper, there are two directions you can fold it. If the crease pokes up, it is called a mountain fold. If it pokes down, it is called a valley fold. One is just the other turned upside down. All origami consists of various combinations of mountain and valley folds. Since this is so, you might wonder why it is necessary to have all these other terms. Why can't you just show where all the creases go on the paper and identify them as mountain and valley folds, and then show how they all go together? Well, you can. The illustration at right shows how that might work for the Swan. However, even a simple fold like this has quite a few creases, and getting them all to go together at once is no mean feat. The situation becomes hopeless with more complicated models—there can be five or ten meters of creases in a bug you can hold in your hand.

In an origami model, mountain and valley folds tend to come in groups of three or four creases. These groups are called combination folds, and they, along with mountain and valley folds, form the building blocks of origami. As it turns out, probably ninety percent of all models can be constructed from about ten or fifteen combination folds. In the other ten percent, there is usually only one small part of the model that requires any special technique, and that part is then manageable.*

A few of the folds in this book require paper that is white on one side and colored on the other. I have used shading on those to indicate the colored side of the paper. The rest of the models can (in fact, should) be folded from paper that is the same color on both sides; however, since commercial origami paper is two-toned, I have indicated at the beginning of the fold which side of the paper should be up to give a predominantly colored model.

In origami, as in other skills, the way to learn is to do. The only way to gain proficiency in reverse folds, for example, is to make a lot of reverse folds. Each of the most important combination folds is introduced in the course of a model in the pages that follow. The combination folds and models get progressively harder, so that by the time you get to the advanced folds in chapter 3, you will be familiar with the basics. Work slowly and carefully, continuously comparing your model with the drawings. As I said before, *read the text*; it is more descriptive in the early models than in later ones. If a term in one of the later models seems unclear, flip back to its first appearance and look at how it was done. Origami builds on past efforts, so be sure to master a model fully before going on to the next.

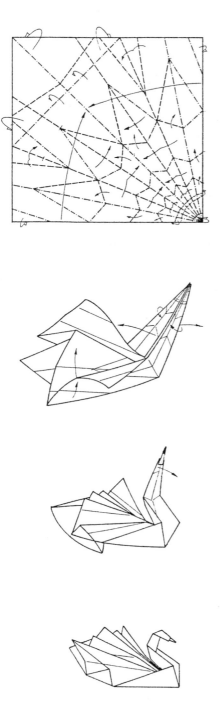

*Not always; most of the first quarter of the Cicada consists of pre-creasing, in preparation for a complex of some 50 creases that all go together at once.

Symbols and Terminology

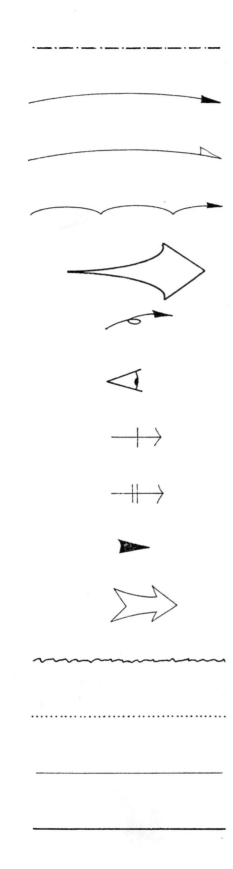

VALLEY FOLD

MOUNTAIN FOLD

FOLD HERE

FOLD BEHIND

FOLD OVER AND OVER

ENLARGED VIEW

TURN OVER

NEXT VIEW FROM HERE

REPEAT ONCE

REPEAT TWICE

SINK

INFLATE

BROKEN-OUT VIEW

HIDDEN FOLD

CREASE

EDGE

HOLD HERE

White-faced Mouse

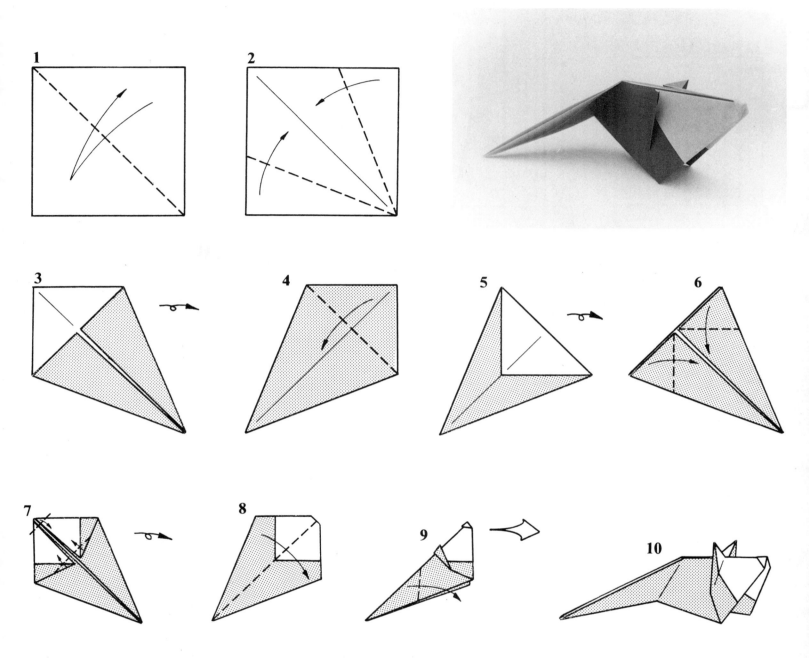

Paper: Use a square, white side up.

1. Valley-fold the paper in half along the diagonal and unfold. A valley fold is always shown by a dashed line indicating the location of the crease and a solid-headed arrow that indicates the motion of the paper. If the arrow returns (as does this one), it means to unfold the paper after you have made the crease. This unfolding is most often done to provide a reference line for future use.

2. Valley-fold both the bottom edge and the right edge of the paper to lie along the diagonal crease made in step 1. The new creases bisect the angle formed by the edges of the paper and the diagonal crease. As it turns out, folding an angle bisector will be a rather common fold.

3. Turn the model over from side to side.

4. Valley-fold the upper right corner down towards the lower left. The crease runs exactly from corner to corner.

5. Turn the model over again.

6. Valley-fold the edges along the short side down to lie upon the center line.

7. At this point, we will begin to identify features on the paper with features of the subject. The upper left corner is the nose. The two loose flaps in the middle of the back are the ears, and the long, skinny point at the bottom is the tail. Valley-fold the tip of the nose down, and the two ears upwards. Turn the model over.

8. Valley-fold the model in half on an existing crease. The crease falls on a natural symmetry line of the model. This happens more often than not.

9. Valley-fold the tail over to one side.

10. Enlarged view (indicated by the hollow expanding arrow). Finished White-faced Mouse.

Duck

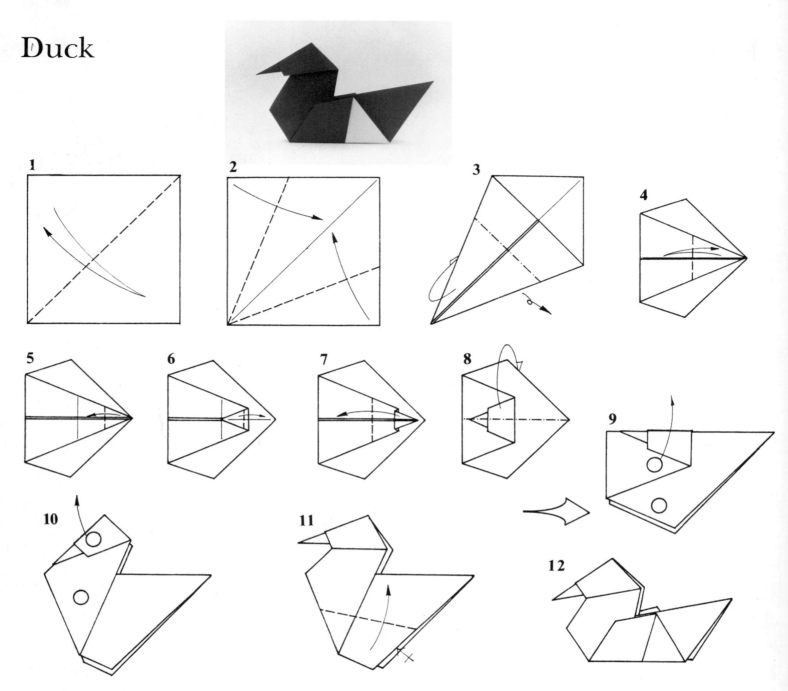

Paper: Use a square, white side up.

1. As in the previous model, fold and unfold the paper in half along the diagonal.

2. Valley-fold the two edges in to lie along the corner-to-corner crease formed in step 1 (also, as in the previous model).

3. Mountain-fold the narrow point behind so that the tip touches the blunt point on the reverse side. A mountain fold is always indicated by a dot-and-dash line (in some texts, two dots and a dash). The direction of folding (away from you) is indicated by a one-sided hollow-headed arrow. Turn the model over.

4. In this example, we are lucky that when we turn the model over, the results of the mountain fold are shown. In later folds with multiple layers, that luxury will not be afforded us. Valley-fold and unfold the narrow corner at the right of the model over to the edge at the left. Make the crease sharp.

5. Valley-fold the tip of the narrow point at the right back to the crease just made.

6. Valley-fold about ¾ of the tip back to the right.

7. Valley-fold the paper back on the crease made in step 4. This makes a head and beak.

8. Mountain-fold the model in half (that is, fold the top half behind). By now, you should recognize the symbols for a mountain or valley fold, so if you see the verbal instructions "fold . . ." (unadorned by the qualifiers "mountain-" or "valley-"), it should be apparent from context or the drawing, or both, which is required.

9. Enlarged view. Hold the model at the positions indicated by the heavy circles—one in each hand. Then pivot the head and neck assembly up to an angle of about 45 degrees. Keeping the head and body in the new orientation, flatten the model out. Form new creases where necessary.

10. Repeat the procedure in step 9, this time holding the neck and pivoting the head before flattening the model. When you finish, the bottom of the head should be parallel to the top edge of the back. These two steps are actually a method of forming reverse folds, which are combination folds you will encounter in the next model.

11. Valley-fold one layer from the bottom upwards. Its edge should coincide with the top of the back. Repeat behind, symmetrically. The short arrow with a slash across it is the repeat arrow, used when a fold or sequence is to be repeated somewhere else on the model. The number of slashes across the tail is equal to the number of times a procedure is to be repeated.

12. Finished Duck.

Fish

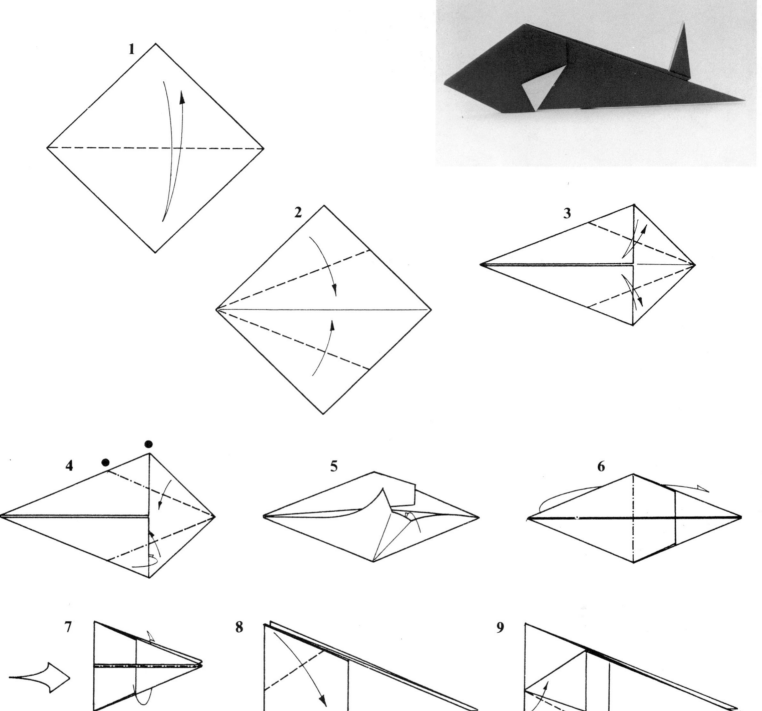

Paper: Use a square, white side up.

1. Fold and unfold the paper along its diagonal.

2. Fold two edges in to lie along the center line, just as in the previous two models.

3. Fold the two remaining raw edges of the square in to lie along the center line; unfold.

4. Reverse-fold the two layers on the existing creases. This is accomplished by valley-folding the lower (partially hidden) layer of the paper, while at the same time making a mountain fold on the upper layer of paper. The "spine" of the crease (the region between the two dots) gets pushed between the two layers, and ends up getting turned inside-out.

5. This shows the upper reverse fold completed and the lower one in progress. There are two types of reverse fold. What is being done in this model is an "inside reverse fold," so named because the flap being folded gets pushed inside the rest of the model. There is also an "outside reverse fold," which we will come to shortly.

6. Mountain-fold the point at the left behind and to the right.

7. Mountain-fold the model in half.

8. Valley-fold one corner down so that simultaneously it touches the bottom edge of the model and its right edge is exactly vertical.

9. Fold the bottom left corner of the model up so that its left edge lies along the crease made in step 8.

10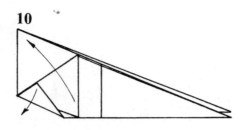

11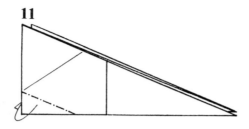

12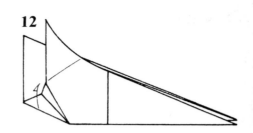

13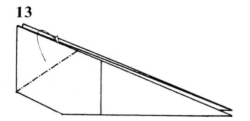

14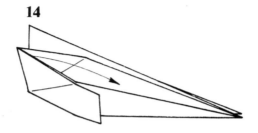

15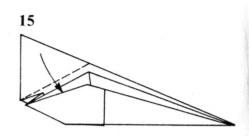

16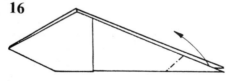

17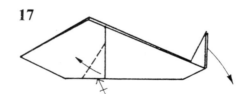

18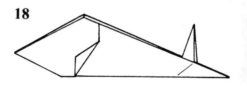

10. Unfold steps 8 and 9.

11. Reverse-fold the bottom corner of the model on the existing crease. As with step 4, turn the crease that's on the upper layer of paper into a mountain fold; then push the spine of the layer inside the model, turning it inside-out.

12. Like this. Flatten the model out.

13. Reverse-fold the upper left-hand corner into the interior of the model in the same way. There are four layers along the top of the model; the point gets pushed between the first and second layer. Note that if you were working from the drawings alone, you couldn't tell whether you should use a reverse fold or a mountain fold. That's why you should always read the text.

14. Reverse fold in progress. We're only doing this to one of the two corners.

15. Tuck the other corner into the pocket formed by the reverse fold. This locks the whole front of the fish together.

16. Reverse-fold both layers of the tail upwards as one, so they are perpendicular to the body. Reverse folds are much easier if the creases are already in place (as they were in steps 4–5 and 11–14), so even though I don't show the pre-creasing as a separate step (from now on, I won't), you should first valley- and mountain-fold where the drawings show the reverse fold should go. Then, push the spine of the reverse fold upwards and allow it to turn inside out. The reverse fold should then fall easily into place.

17. Valley-fold the flap on the side of the body out to make a fin. Repeat symmetrically on the back side. Undo one layer of the reverse fold to split the tail.

18. Finished Fish.

Swan

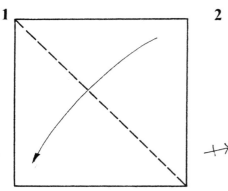

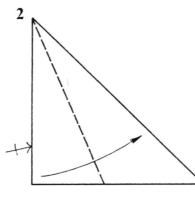

1

2

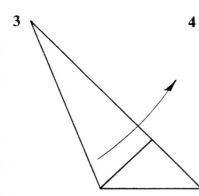

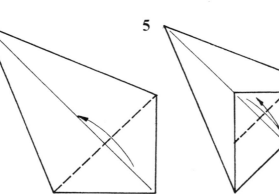

3

4

5

6

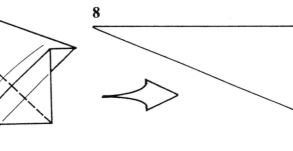

7

8

9

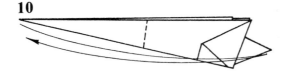

10

11

Paper: Use a square, white side up.

1. Valley-fold the square in half along the diagonal.

2. Bring the left edge over to lie along the diagonal. Repeat behind.

3. Fold the top layer upwards. That is, undo the fold made in step 1.

4. Fold the blunt triangle upwards so that its tip lies along the center line, and the crease runs from corner to corner.

5. Fold the tip of the blunt triangle down to the crease just made, and unfold.

6. Fold the tip of the blunt triangle back down, so that the crease made in step 5 and the edge made in step 4 line up.

7. Valley-fold the model in half.

8. Enlarged view. Pivot the small triangle protruding from the right side downward about thirty degrees (the exact angle isn't critical). This is done the same way we made the head and neck of the Duck; pivot it down, and flatten the model out, forming new creases as necessary.

9. Valley-fold the bottom edge (one layer only) up to lie along the back. Repeat behind, symmetrically.

10. Fold the skinny point (soon to be the head and neck) over to touch the tail; crease, and unfold.

11. Form a valley fold that connects points A and B. Crease and unfold.

12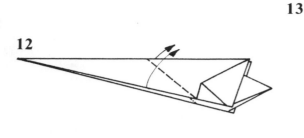

13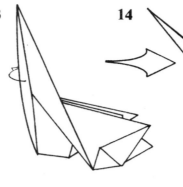

14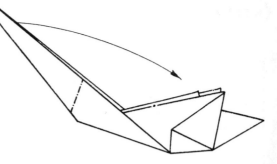

15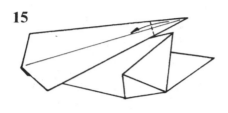

16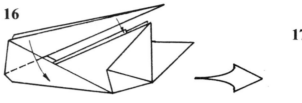

17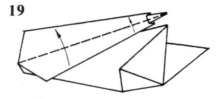

18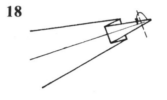

19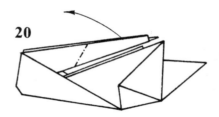

20

21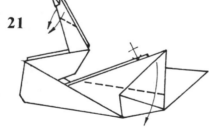

22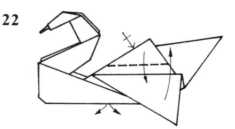

23

12. Outside-reverse-fold the neck. To make an outside reverse fold, the edges of the flap being folded are wrapped up around the spine of the flap. The difference between an outside reverse fold and an inside reverse fold is that in the former, the inside gets wrapped *around* the rest of the model, while in the latter, the outside gets pushed *inside* the rest of the model. As far as diagrams go, an outside reverse fold is indicated by valley folds (as here); an inside reverse fold is indicated by mountain folds. And, as with the inside reverse fold, it is much easier if you pre-crease the paper with valley and mountain folds before trying the reverse fold.

13. This shows the fold in progress.

14. Enlarged view. Inside reverse-fold the neck back to lie parallel to the back of the swan.

15. Open the front of the neck out flat.

16. Fold about ¼ of the neck back on itself.

17. Fold about ¾ of the tip back up on itself.

18. Blunt the tip by folding the last little bit back down.

19. Close the neck back up with a valley fold.

20. Inside reverse-fold the head forward so that it is at right angles to the back.

21. Outside reverse-fold the head downward. Fold the tips of the wings downward, both front and behind.

22. Fold the next layer of paper down over the wings in front and behind. The central point remains upright. Open out the bottom of the swan and spread the layers of the back.

23. Finished Swan.

Cap

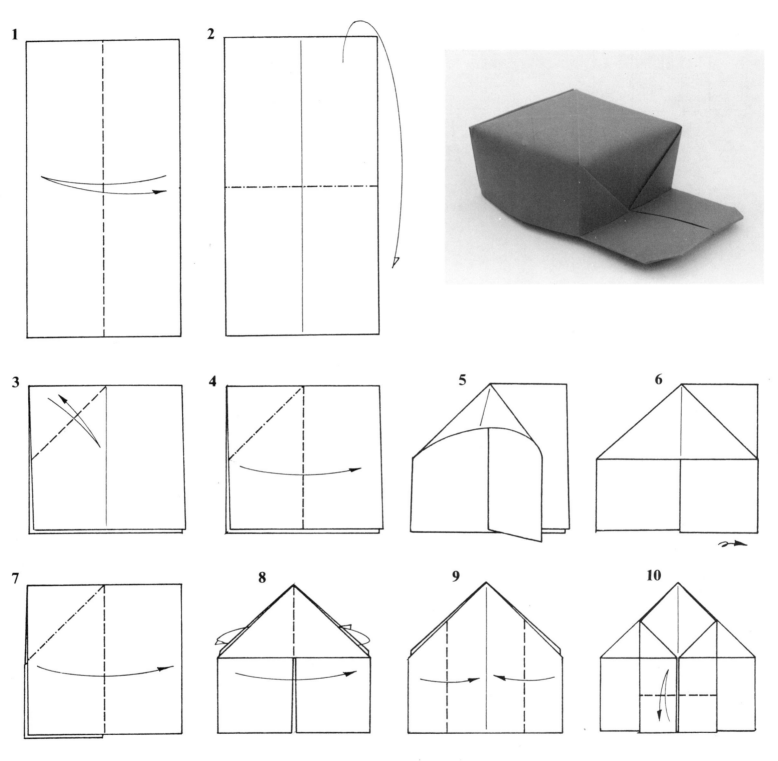

Paper: Use a 1:2 rectangle, colored side up.

1. Fold the paper in half the long way, crease and unfold.

2. Mountain-fold the paper in half the other way.

3. Fold the upper left edge down to lie along the center line; crease and unfold.

4. Fold a single layer from the left over to the right on the existing vertical crease; in the process, the corner gets stretched out. Squash it down, symmetrically. This is called a squash fold.

5. Squash fold in progress.

6. Squash fold completed. Turn the paper over from side to side.

7. Squash-fold the remaining layer in exactly the same way.

8. Valley-fold one layer from left to right in front. This is called a book fold, because the action resembles turning pages of a book. Also, fold one layer from right to left in back, to keep the same number of layers on both sides.

9. Fold the left and right edges (one layer only) in to the center line.

10. Fold the flap at the bottom of the model up to touch the raw edges in the middle of the model; unfold.

11

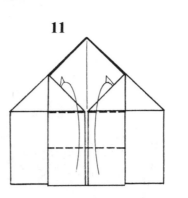

12

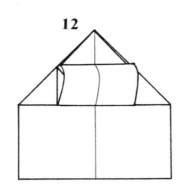

13

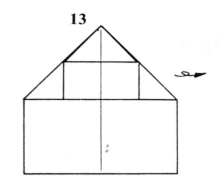

14

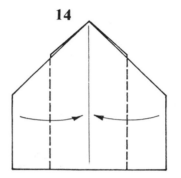

15

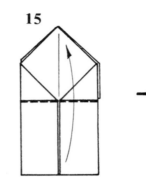

16

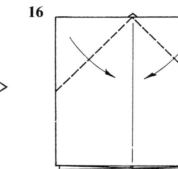

17

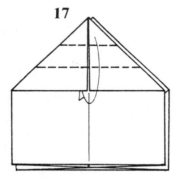

18

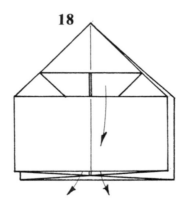

19

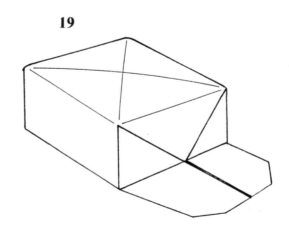

11. Fold the same flap up as far as it will go, and tuck it into the two triangular pockets illustrated.

12. In progress.

13. Like so. Turn the model over from side to side.

14. Fold the edges of the model in to the center line, as in step 9.

15. Fold the flap at the bottom as far up as it will go.

16. Enlarged view. Fold the two corners to the center line.

17. Fold the point (one layer only) down in thirds; tuck the last third underneath the layers shown.

18. Fold the brim down and open up the inside of the cap.

19. Finished Cap.

Shark

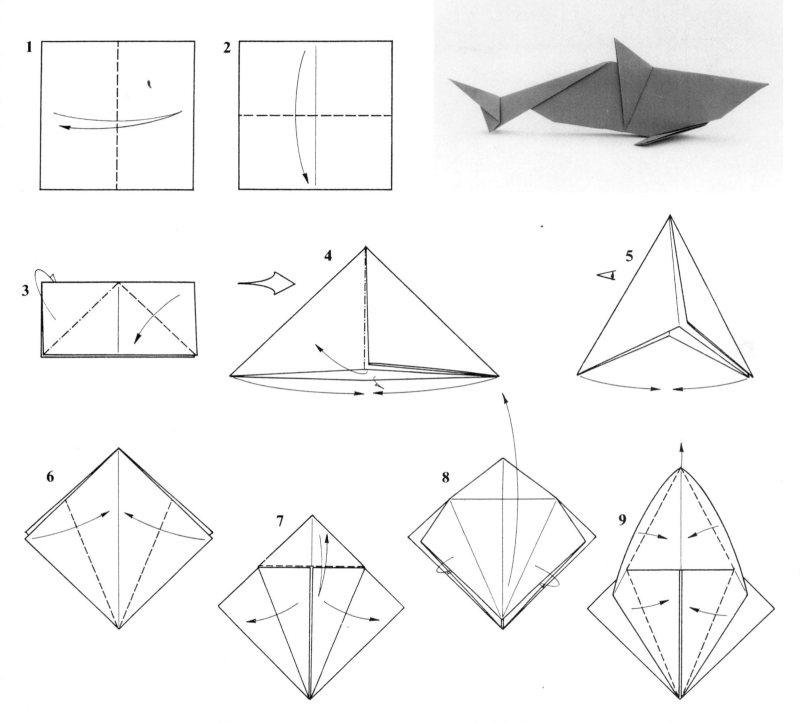

Paper: Use a square, white side up.

1. Book-fold the paper in half vertically; crease and unfold.

2. Fold the paper in half horizontally.

3. Mountain-fold the upper left corner behind. Valley-fold the upper right corner toward you.

4. Enlarged view. Spread the layers in the middle apart, and bring the two corners together.

5. In progress. The little "eye" next to the drawing means that the next view will be drawn from this vantage point. Alternatively, you may think of it as a command to rotate the paper about an axis lying in the plane of the page. It will appear quite often in the three-dimensional folds, which require drawings from several angles.

6. Flatten the paper out so that two flaps lie on the right and two on the left. This shape appears quite often in origami, and is called the Preliminary Fold. Fold two raw edges in to lie along the center line.

7. Fold the top, thick point down over the flaps folded in step 6. Unfold all three.

8. Petal-fold the front flap of the model. To do this, lift a single layer of paper up along the horizontal crease while holding down the remaining points at the bottom of the model. The edges of the paper get dragged in toward the middle.

9. Petal-fold in progress. The edges will tend to fall naturally on the creases made in step 6 (although the upper ones must be converted from mountain to valley folds, as shown here). Flatten the model out.

15

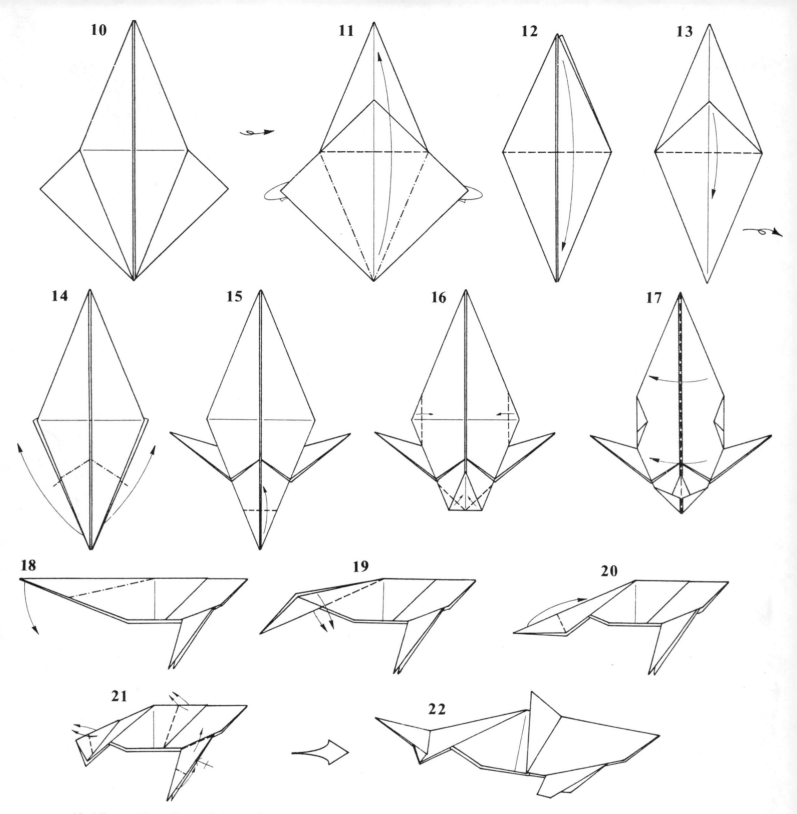

10. Like so. Turn the model over from side to side.

11. Petal-fold this side the same way. From now on, I'll only show the creases as they appear in the final petal fold. However, just as with reverse folds, you will probably have an easier time of it if you pre-crease the paper first (i.e., repeat steps 6 and 7) before you do the petal fold.

12. Like so. This shape also is very common in origami. It is the basis for the traditional Japanese Flapping Bird and Crane, and is widely known as the Bird Base. Fold one flap down.

13. Fold the thick, stubby point down as far as it will go. Turn the model over from side to side.

14. Reverse-fold the two points at the bottom out to the sides. (I didn't say which kind of reverse fold to use, but you can see from the mountain-fold line that they are inside reverse folds.)

15. Fold the tip of the bottom upwards.

16. Fold the sides in and the corners of the bottom in.

17. Fold the model in half.

18. Reverse-fold the tail downwards (inside reverse fold).

19. Fold one layer in front down, and one layer behind down, so that the tail gets wrapped around the body.

20. Outside-reverse-fold the tip of the tail upwards. This can be done simply by opening the tail out flat, valley-folding the tip upwards, and then closing the tail back up again.

21. Outside-reverse-fold both the tail and the fin on the back. Reverse-fold the tips of the pectoral fins and valley-fold the fins out to the side.

22. Enlarged view. Finished Shark.

Kangaroo

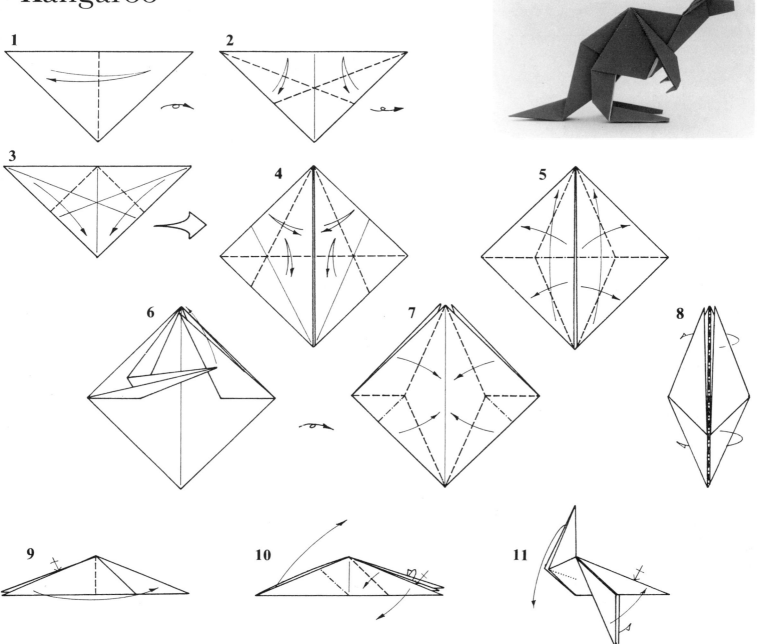

Paper: Use an isosceles right triangle, colored side up. You can make one by cutting a square in half along the diagonal.

1. Fold the triangle in half vertically, crease and unfold. Turn the paper over from side to side.

2. Crease the angle bisectors as shown (that is, fold the short edges of the triangle up to lie along the top edge, and unfold).

3. Fold the acute points of the triangle down to the right angle.

4. Enlarged view. There are now two flaps, each of which is an isosceles right triangle with a crease bisecting one of the vertices. Crease the angle bisectors of the remaining two vertices on each triangle (for a total of four creases). The three bisectors in each triangle should intersect at a single point.

5. On each flap, valley-fold all three angle bisectors simultaneously, and bring the bottom corners up to the top. In the process of flattening things out, the mountain folds shown here will form. This sequence is called a rabbit ear. It will always consist of three valley folds and one mountain fold radiating from a common point, and usually the valley folds run to the three points of a triangle while the mountain fold terminates on an edge.

6. Rabbit ear in progress. Flatten things out and turn the model over.

7. Fold two more rabbit ears. Note that the crease patterns are almost the same as those of step 5, but now the outer points get brought into the center of the model. As with past combination folds, it is much easier if you first pre-crease the three valley folds.

8. Mountain-fold the model in half vertically.

9. Valley-fold one layer all the way over to the right. Repeat behind.

10. Reverse-fold the remaining point on the left so that it points straight up. Valley-fold the top layer on the right so that the crease lies directly on top of the edge of the shorter point underneath. Repeat behind.

11. Reverse-fold the vertical point back downwards. The dotted line is a hidden line and indicates that a crease lies beneath the visible layers of paper. Here it shows where the creases in the reverse fold belong. Unfold the two valley folds made in step 10.

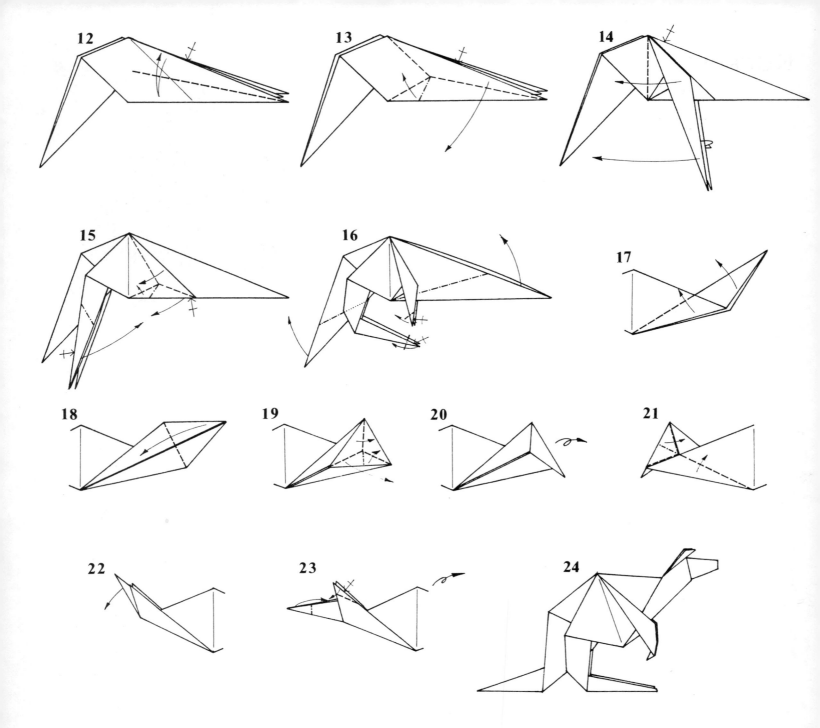

12. Enlarged view. Crease the angle bisector on the top two layers of paper. It is not possible to flatten out the crease all the way across the model (that is, you can't "resolve" the crease). This is indicated in the drawing by the dashed line ending abruptly, as it does here, rather than terminating on an edge. Repeat behind.

13. Form another rabbit ear with the long skinny flap. Two of the three valley folds are existing creases; the third connects the intersection of the other two with the corner of the belly, as shown. When you make the rabbit ear and flatten it out, the mountain fold will fall into place. Repeat behind.

14. Valley-fold both rabbit ears over to the left of the model. Repeat behind.

15. Rabbit-ear the two shorter points to the right. The rightmost valley fold is an angle bisector. The upper valley fold is one-third of the angle between the edge of the flap and the vertical crease. The last valley fold connects the intersection of the first two with the corner of the belly; the mountain fold falls into place when you flatten it out. Reverse-fold about two-thirds of the legs to the right. Repeat behind.

16. Reverse-fold the tail so its bottom and the bottoms of the feet line up. Reverse-fold the tips of the rear legs to blunt them, and the front legs to give paws to the kangaroo. Reverse-fold the neck upwards.

17. Open the neck out flat.

18. Fold the tip of the head down; the crease runs from corner to corner.

19. Rabbit-ear the tip; the valley folds are all angle bisectors.

20. Like so. Turn the model over from side to side.

21. Rabbit-ear the neck as shown, folding all the layers together as one.

22. Pivot the head (the longer flap) downwards. Flatten out the model, forming new creases where necessary.

23. Valley-fold the ears forward. Reverse-fold the tip of the head to blunt the muzzle. Turn the model over from side to side.

24. Finished Kangaroo.

Rocket

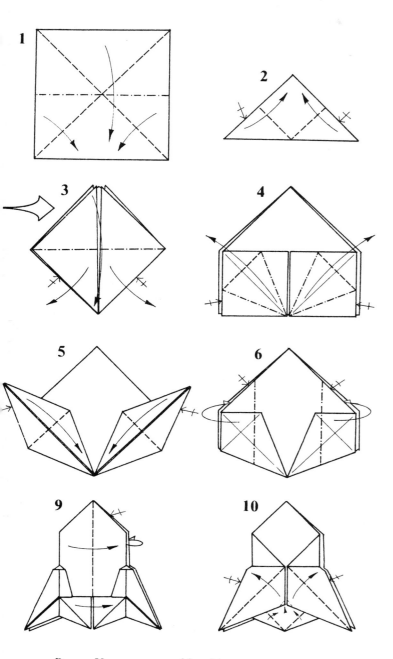

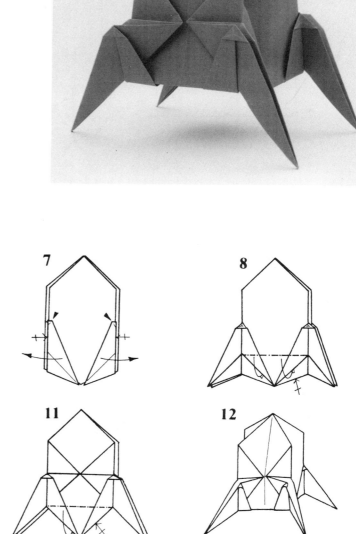

Paper: Use a square, white side up.

1. Crease the diagonals with valley folds and the horizontal bisector with a mountain fold. Using these creases, bring the middle of the sides and the top of the square together to meet at the middle of the bottom.

2. The result is shown here; there are two flaps on the left and two on the right. This shape, like the Preliminary Fold, is a common one in origami. It is called the Waterbomb Base. (You can also get it by turning a Preliminary Fold inside-out.) Fold one point each from the left and the right up to the top of the model. Repeat behind.

3. Enlarged view. Squash-fold the points symmetrically. Repeat behind.

4. Petal-fold all four of the points. As when we made a Bird Base, the petal fold will be much easier if you pre-crease first.

5. Valley-fold all four points back down to the base of the model.

6. Mountain-fold the edges of the model into the interior, as far as they will go. Repeat behind.

7. Allow the four points at the bottom of the model to swing outward. Tiny gussets will form where the heavy black arrowheads are pointing. Squash them flat. Repeat behind.

8. Mountain-fold the triangular region up inside the model. Repeat behind.

9. Book-fold. That is, fold one layer over in front, and one layer the other direction in back.

10. Fold the lower edges of the kite-shaped regions upwards on the valley folds. In the process, the edges of the triangular point at the bottom of the model will be dragged upwards, forming a gusset that will need to be squashed. This maneuver—in which one valley fold requires a squash fold to go with it—is called a swivel fold. (The tiny gussets made in step 7 must also be formed in this example, but they are not part of a usual swivel fold.) Repeat behind.

11. Mountain-fold the triangles into the interior of the model, as in step 8. Open out the bottom of the model and spread the four legs.

12. Finished Rocket.

Seated Lady

1

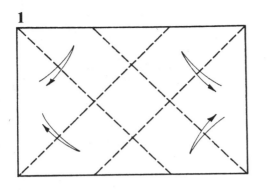

2

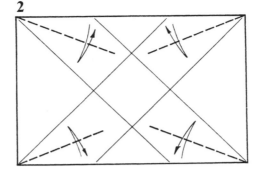

3

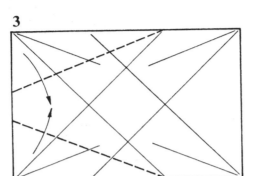

4

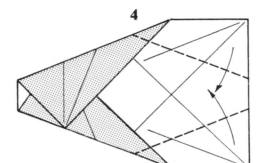

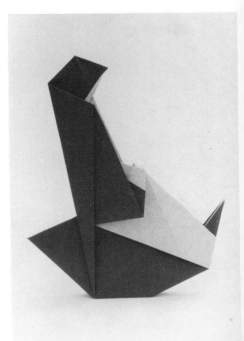

5

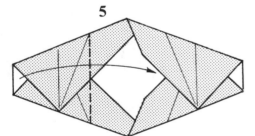

6

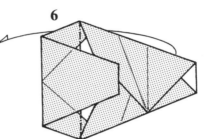

7

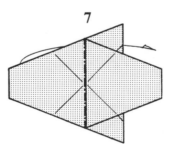

8

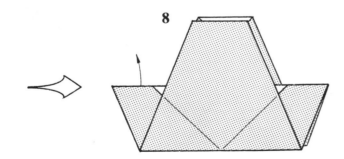

9

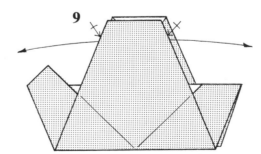

Paper: Use a 1:1.5 rectangle, white side up.

1. Bisect each of the four corners with a valley fold. Crease and unfold.

2. Form each of the creases shown by folding the long edges to the diagonal creases made in step 1. It is not necessary to resolve the creases (that is, to continue each crease all the way to an edge).

3. Fold the left-hand corners in so that the top and bottom edges lie along the diagonal creases on the left side of the model.

4. Do the same on the right side of the model.

5. Fold the left third of the model over to the right. This can be accomplished by folding the left edge over so that it touches the intersection of the two edges on the right.

6. Mountain-fold the right half of the model behind.

7. Mountain-fold the rear flap back to the right so that it lines up with the upper layer.

8. Enlarged view (and rotated a quarter-turn). Pull the trapped layers of paper as far out as they will go.

9. Reach inside the model and pull the original corners of the rectangle as far out as they will come. A mountain fold will tend to form on the creases made in step 2. Help them along, and flatten the model out, letting new creases appear where they naturally fall.

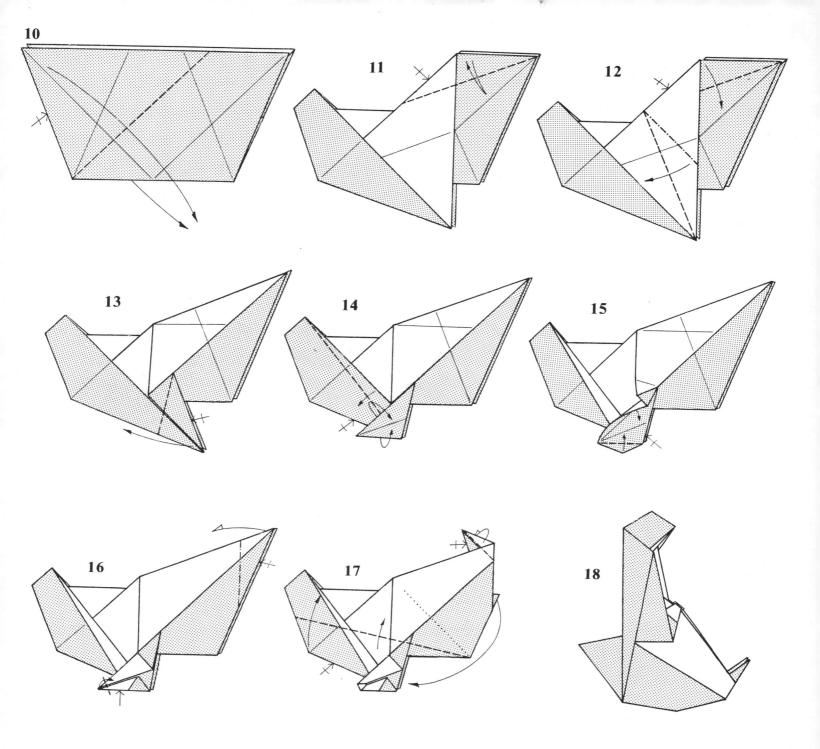

10. Valley-fold the upper left corners down to the lower right as far as they will go (both front and rear).

11. Crease the angle bisector. Repeat behind.

12. Swivel-fold. The rightward valley fold already exists; the other valley fold connects the bottom point with the intersection of the first crease and the edge of the paper. When both valley folds are made and the model is flattened out, the mountain fold will form in the right place. (Both swivel folds and rabbit ears are like this; if all the valley folds are in place, the mountain folds appear on their own when you flatten the model out.)

13. Valley-fold the bottom point up so that its edge is aligned with the raw edge of the paper, as shown in the next step. Repeat behind.

14. Wrap the layers of paper from the back side of the small point to the front side. The upper layer comes free easily; you will have to make the long, skinny valley fold to free up the lower layer. Repeat behind.

15. This shows the wrap in progress.

16. Wrap fold completed. Valley-fold the tip of the lower point over to the right. Mountain-fold the two-colored points at the right back to the left. Repeat behind.

17. Valley-fold the irregular shape at the bottom of the model upwards. The valley fold runs to the corner shown at the right; the leftmost corner of the flap comes up to touch the white portion of the model. Reverse-fold the blunt point that is barely visible at the right down towards the bottom. The dotted line is a hidden line; it shows where the reverse fold is occurring underneath the other layers. Finally, mountain-fold the feet (at the upper right) in half. Repeat behind, and rotate the model by a quarter-turn clockwise.

18. Finished Seated Lady.

Nun

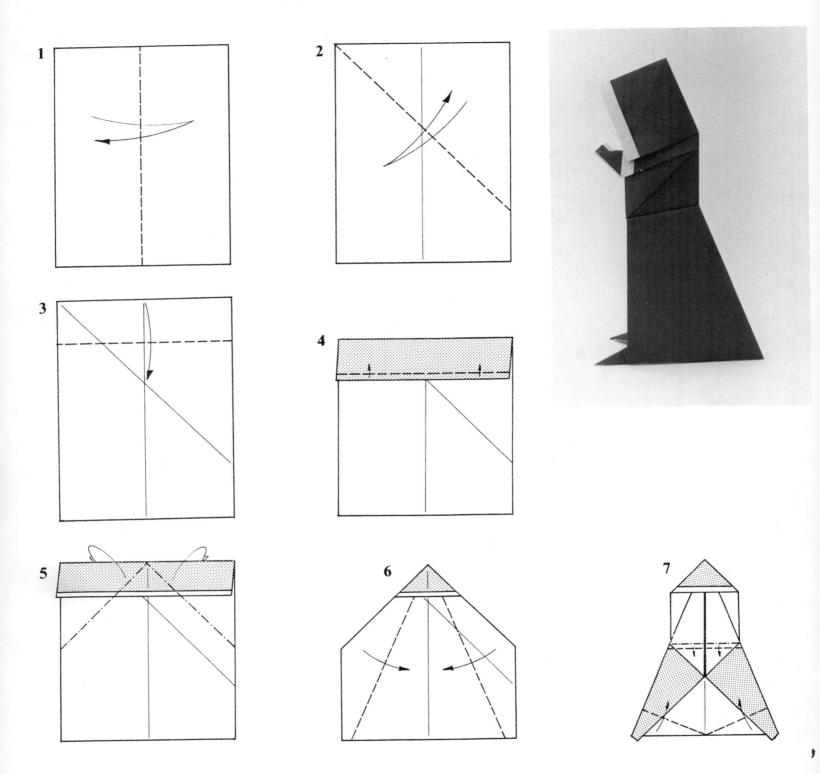

Paper: Use a 1:1.294 rectangle (e.g., an 8½ by 11 inch sheet), white side up.

1. Fold and unfold the paper in half vertically.

2. Fold and unfold one of the diagonals.

3. Fold the top edge down to touch the intersection of the previous two creases.

4. Fold a small portion (about ⅙) of the flap back up to create a white border on a colored background.

5. Mountain-fold the corners behind.

6. Valley-fold the new edges in to lie along the center line. The valley folds extend up under the little "cap," all the way to the tip of the point.

7. Form a mountain and valley fold, parallel to each other at the waist. This is called a pleat. Valley-fold the bottom corners upwards; the creases are perpendicular to the outside edges of the model.

22

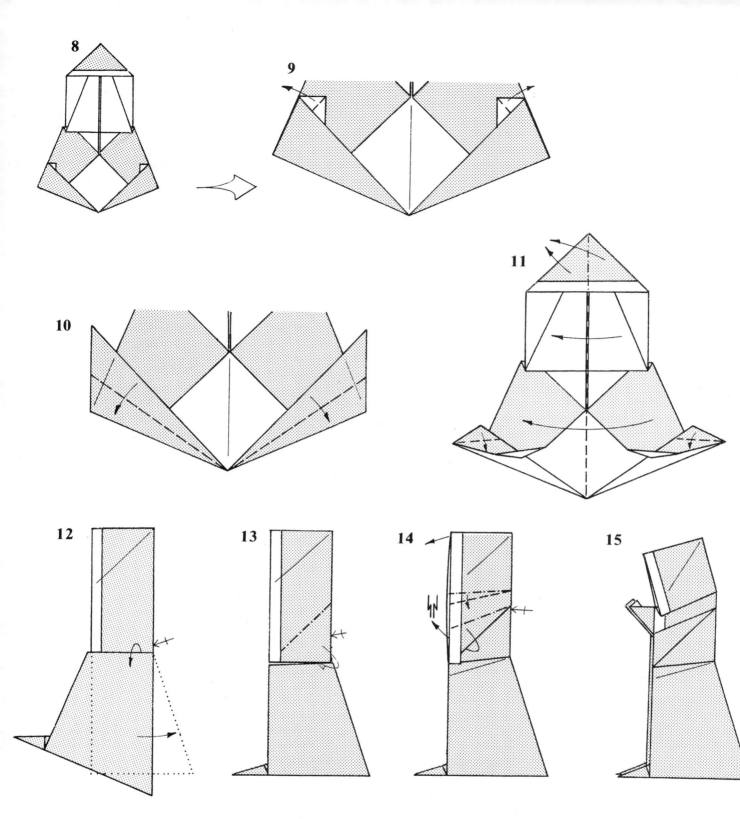

8. Like so.

9. Enlarged view. Pull the corners to the outside, as in step 9 of the Seated Lady. In this case, however, you will have to form creases for the valley folds that run to the corners; they don't already exist.

10. Valley-fold the triangles along an angle bisector. Small gussets will form along their upper edge, as they did in step 7 of the Rocket.

11. Narrow the feet with valley folds. Valley-fold the model in half, but pull the middle of the little "cap" at the top out of the inside of the model as you flatten it out.

12. Untuck the layers trapped in the pleat. Pivot the lower

portion of the model towards the right so that the left side of the upper and lower portions of the model are aligned. Flatten the model out.

13. Reverse-fold the corner shown. Repeat behind.

14. The two mirror-image zigzag lines to the left of the model indicate a crimp fold. Do this with mountain and valley folds made like a pleat, with their mirror image on the other side of the model (so an edge-on view looks like the double zigzag line). Mountain-fold the arms underneath as far as they will go. Repeat behind.

15. Finished Nun.

Vulture

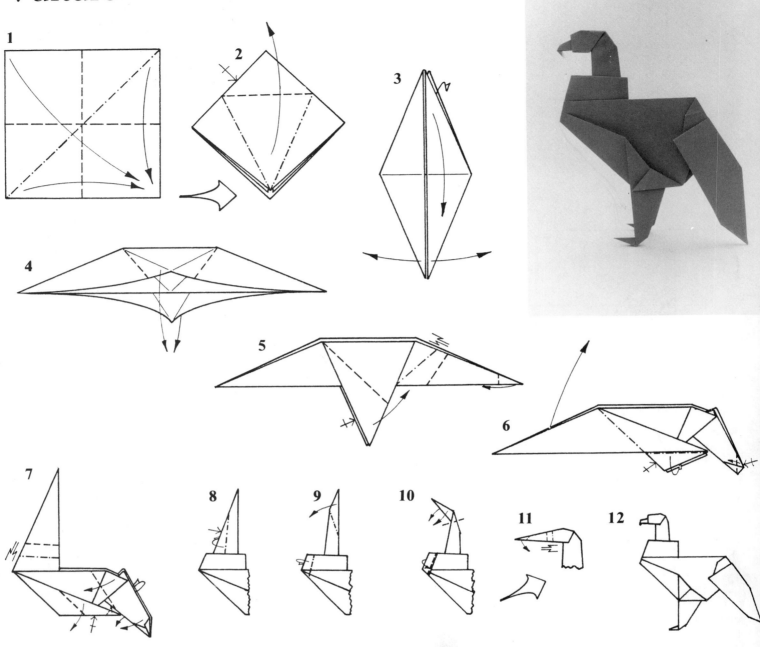

Paper: Use a square, white side up.

1. Divide the paper in half vertically and horizontally with valley folds, and crease a mountain fold along the diagonal. Bring the four corners together. This is another way of making a Preliminary Fold.

2. Rotate the model so that the four corners of the square are at the bottom. Petal-fold the corner in front and behind, to make a Bird Base.

3. Bring down the two points at the top. Grasp the other two points at the bottom, one in each hand, and stretch them as far apart as they will go.

4. Like so. Flatten the model out; the valley folds shown will form naturally.

5. Valley-fold the bottom points over to the right as far as possible. Crimp the point at the right. This crimp is most easily accomplished as a sequence of two reverse folds; first, do an inside reverse fold where the mountain fold symbol is. Then, do another inside reverse fold that is parallel to it. It will be even easier if you pre-crease the mountain and valley folds before you try the reverse folds. Finally, outside-reverse-fold the tip of the tail (at the right).

6. Inside-reverse-fold the left point upwards. The two short points pointing to the right at the bottom of the model are the legs. Reverse-fold the lower half of the leg; repeat behind. Valley-fold the corner of the tail; repeat behind.

7. Crimp the neck (the vertical point at the left). This, too, is most easily done as a pair of inside reverse folds. Valley-fold the legs downwards. Outside-reverse-fold the tail.

8. Mountain-fold the edges of the neck into the interior of the model. Tiny gussets will form at the base (as in a swivel fold); flatten them out.

9. Reverse-fold the top of the neck to form a head. Mountain-fold the edge of one layer of the neck into the interior of the model.

10. Outside-reverse-fold the head. Valley-fold the other edge of the neck into the interior of the model.

11. Enlarged view of the head. Crimp the beak (using two reverse folds) and reverse-fold the tip of the beak downward to give it a hook.

12. Finished Vulture.

Songbird

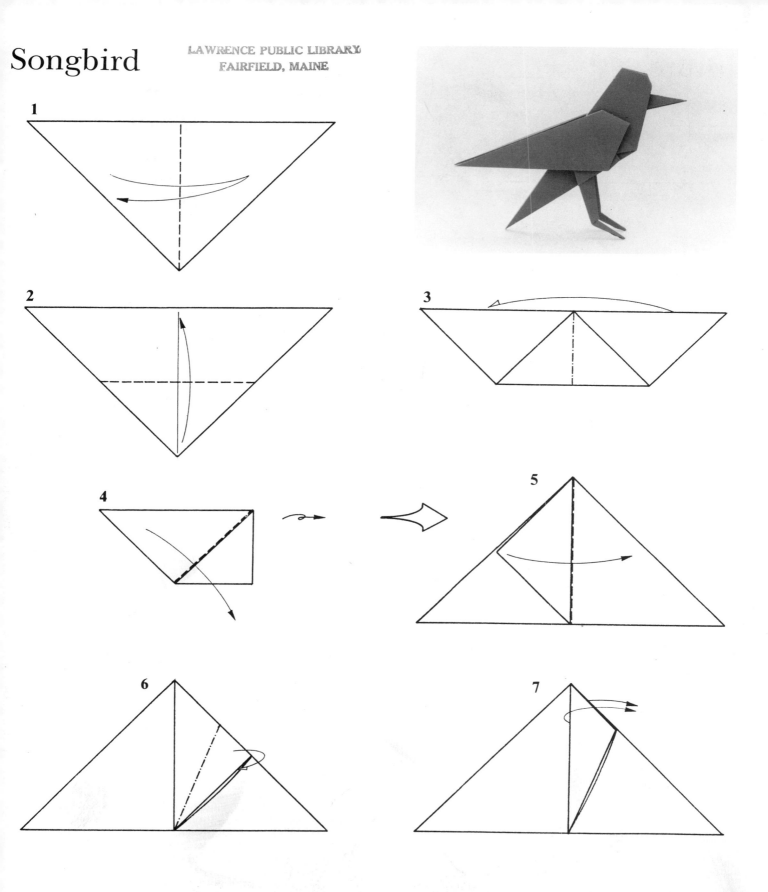

Paper: Use an isosceles right triangle, colored side up.
1. Fold the triangle in half vertically. Unfold.
2. Fold the bottom point of the triangle up to touch the top edge.
3. Mountain-fold the right half over behind the left half.
4. Valley-fold one layer down over the raw edge of the paper. Turn the model over and rotate it to the orientation of figure 5.

5. Valley-fold the blunt point over to the right.
6. Reverse-fold the indicated edge into the interior of the model along an angle bisector.
7. Unwrap the indicated layer of paper. You will have to let the model come partially unfolded to do this. The layer gets turned inside-out, and in this respect resembles an outside reverse fold.

25

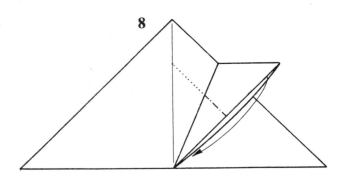

8

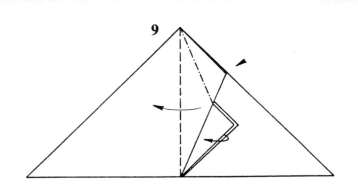

9

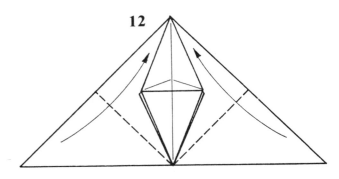

10

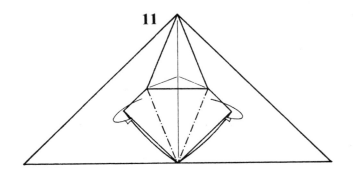

11

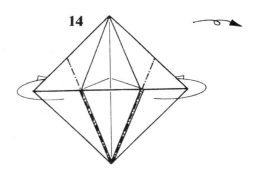

12

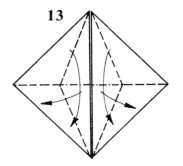

13

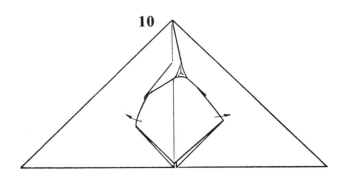

14

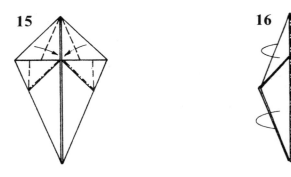

15

16

8. Reverse-fold the corner shown down to the bottom of the model. As the hidden line shows, the reverse fold extends up into the model to the center line.

9. Spread the two blunt flaps in the lower third of the model and squash the point indicated by the heavy black arrowhead. This maneuver is called a spread-squash. The spread-squash will easily fall into place if you first spread the two bottom points as far as they will go . . .

10. . . . like this; the top point will rise up off of your folding surface. Then, as you hold the two lower points down, start pushing the top point down as well. A tiny triangular region in the middle of the point will flatten out as shown here; as you spread the three corners of the region to be spread-squashed, the flat region will grow. Eventually, the entire region will be flat. You can then smooth out the layers and make all the new creases sharp.

11. The result looks like this. Reverse-fold the edges into the model. (Notice that the creases look a lot like the ones you used when you made a Bird Base. That suggests that you can make these reverse folds by petal-folding the corner of the paper, then bringing the petal fold back down.)

12. Fold the two large points up to cover the region you were just working on.

13. Rabbit-ear the two flaps back down to the bottom of the model. The three valley folds are all angle bisectors.

14. Mountain-fold the edges behind. Turn the model over from side to side.

15. Reverse-fold the remaining edges. Each vertical valley fold will fall into place if you make the other two folds and flatten the paper out. We could have also obtained this result from step 14 using rabbit ears.

16. Mountain-fold the model in half.

17 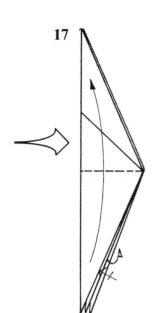 **18** 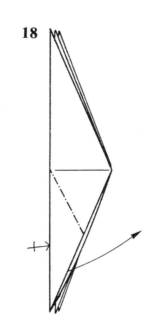 **19** 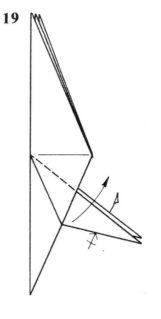 **20**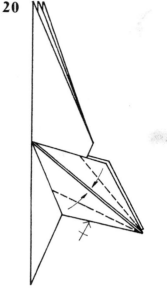

21 **22** **23**

24 **25** **26**

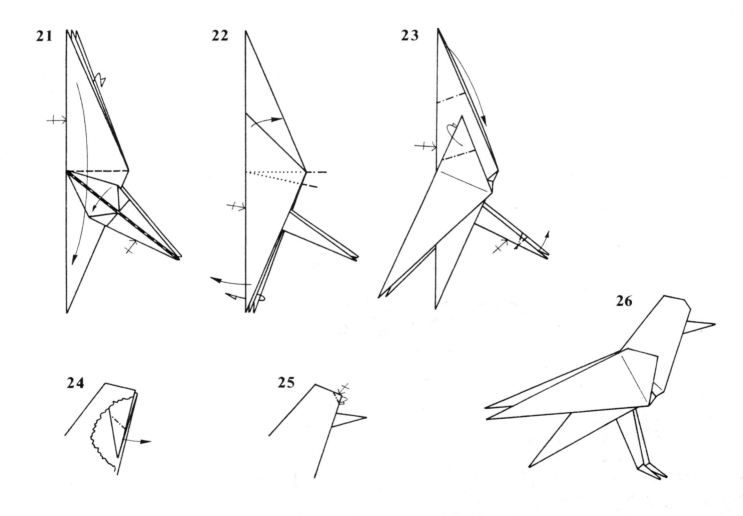

17. Enlarged view. Fold one layer from the bottom up to the top of the model; repeat behind.

18. Reverse-fold the indicated point forward. Repeat behind.

19. Open the point out flat. Repeat behind.

20. Narrow the point by valley-folding its edges in to the center line. Repeat behind.

21. Fold the point in half again, and fold the point from the top of the model down over it. Repeat behind.

22. Pivot the wing (the long point) to the left (moving the shoulder to the right). Flatten out the new creases.

23. Reverse-fold the head down inside the model. Mountain-fold the tip of the shoulder behind. Crimp the feet forwards.

24. The jagged line indicates that this is a broken-out view—a view of something that would normally be hidden. It is shown as if the paper in front were torn away. Reverse-fold the hidden point shown here outward to form a beak.

25. Mountain-fold the corners of the head into the model.

26. Finished Songbird.

King Tut

Paper: Use a square, white side up.

1. Crease one diagonal with a valley fold. Valley-fold the paper in half along the other.

2. Valley-fold one corner down; mountain-fold the other behind.

3. Spread the inner bottom points apart, and bring the sides together.

4. This is another way of forming the Waterbomb Base. Squash-fold one corner.

5. Petal-fold the corner.

6. Fold the flap back down.

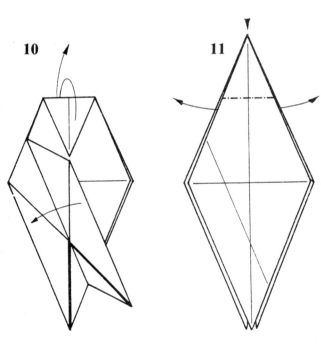

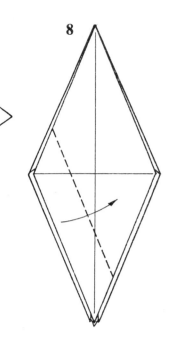

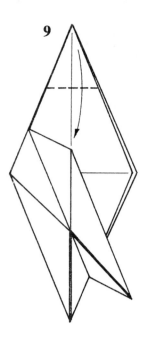

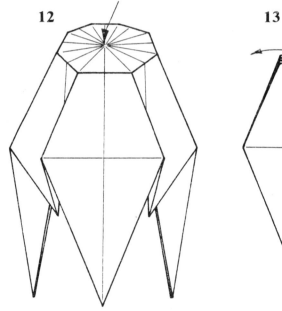

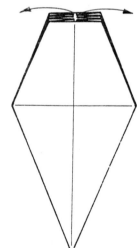

7. Repeat steps 4–6 on the other three flaps.

8. Enlarged view. This is another common shape, called the Frog Base. Fold one flap along a line parallel to the edge, so that the left corner touches the center line.

9. Fold the thick top point down to touch the corner.

10. Undo the point, and fold it behind on the same crease. Unfold everything to step 8.

11. Sink, or invert, the top point. This is done by spreading the layers of the model apart and flattening out the region to be sunk. You can facilitate the sink by making a series of

mountain folds all the way around the region to be sunk (the mountain folds should be made where the creases of steps 9 and 10 are).

12. This shows the sink in progress. Push the center of the sink fold down into the inside of the model and close the model back up again. The top edges of the sink will be pleated.

13. Finished sink. Reverse-fold the central pair of pleats to the outside of the model.

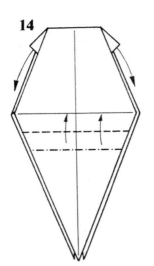 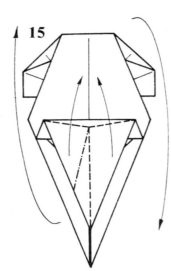 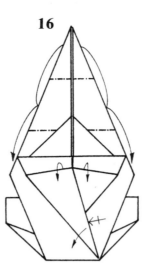 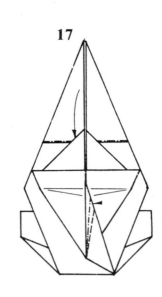

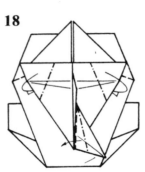 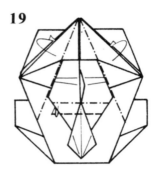 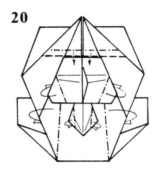

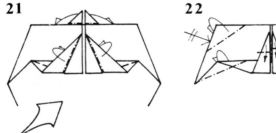 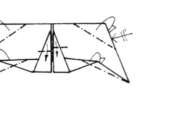 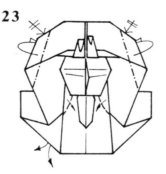 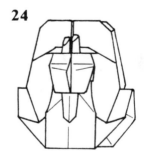

14. Pull the same pleats as far down as they will go. Pleat the flap at the bottom.

15. Form an asymmetrical rabbit ear in the pleated flap. In this case, there are no reference creases (except the vertical valley fold); you'll have to use your judgment for the location of the rest of the creases. Rotate the model 180 degrees.

16. Reverse-fold the points at the top of the model down, and reverse-fold them down again inside themselves. Pull the layer of paper trapped behind the rabbit ear out on the left. Repeat on the right.

17. Sink the remaining point at the tip of the model down inside itself. Crimp the point emanating from the center line of the model. The crimp forms a nose and beard.

18. Reverse-fold the edges of the head. Squash-fold the beard.

19. Mountain-fold the edges of the head. Pleat the lower face.

20. Narrow the face, beard and chest with mountain folds. Pleat the two points above the head down over it.

21. Reverse-fold the remaining tiny points on top of the headdress down into the model. Swivel-fold the two lower points, which become ornaments.

22. Mountain-fold all of the corners of the headdress, and the corners of the ornaments. Fold their tips down to form heads (they are, respectively, a vulture and an asp).

23. Mountain-fold all of the edges of the headdress into the interior of the model. Pinch the beard from side to side. Spread the front and back of the base of the mask.

24. Finished King Tut.

Chapter 2 introduced the most common combination folds. Now, you will put them to use. Of course, there are an infinite number of more complicated sequences, but they don't occur as regularly as the ones listed in the previous chapter. This next group of folds is more difficult than the last. It includes several procedures that require some dexterity. The paper may not be lying flat at the end of a step, or a crease may not be resolved. In some folds, you may have to bring five or ten creases together at once. Nevertheless, everything is spelled out in the words and diagrams, and the results will be well worth your efforts.

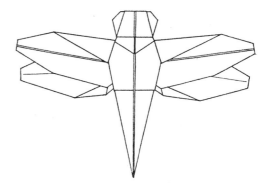

Gerbil

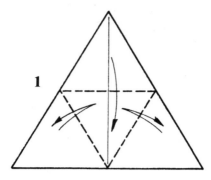

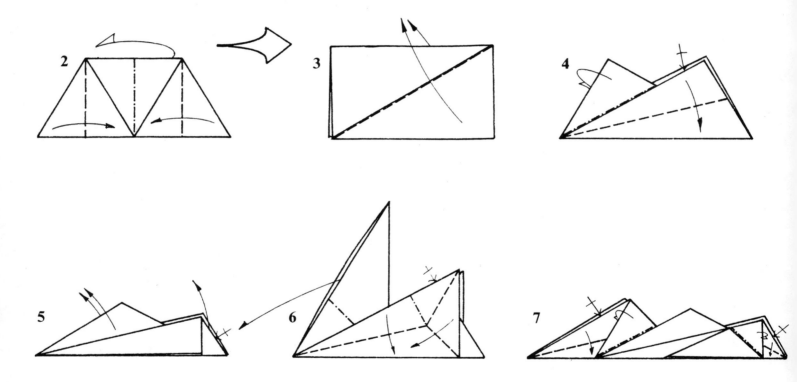

Paper: Use an equilateral triangle, colored side up.

1. Fold each corner to the midpoint of the opposite side. Crease and unfold. Leave the top point folded down.

2. Fold each of the sides in to the center line. Mountain-fold the model in half and rotate 90 degrees counterclockwise.

3. Enlarged view. Valley-fold the lower right corner up, both in front and in back.

4. Reverse-fold the upper left point down into the model. Valley-fold one layer down so that its edge lies along the base of the model. Repeat behind.

5. Release the single layer of paper covering the top of the model, as if you were unfolding an outside reverse fold. Unfold the two original corners of the triangle that are at the right of the model.

6. Reverse-fold the top point (the tail) downward. Rabbit-ear the indicated flaps, both front and rear.

7. Reverse-fold the edges of the head (right) and tail (left) downward. Repeat behind.

8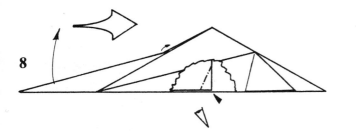

9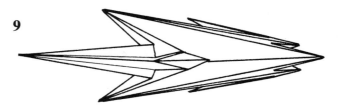

10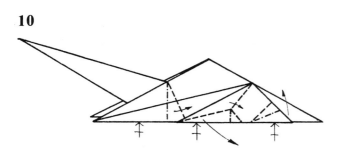

11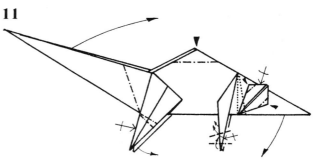

12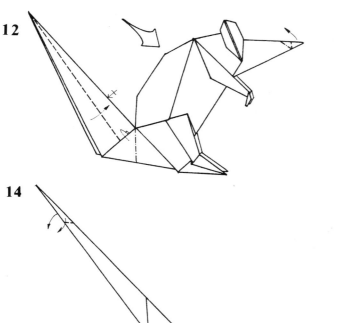

13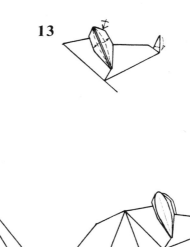

14

15

8. Enlarged view. Pivot the tail upwards. It will be necessary to sink the indicated corner into the interior of the model. The jagged line indicates that this is a broken-out view, as if you had ripped a hole in the paper to see the layers underneath.

9. This is a view of the edges of the bottom of the model, as seen from the vantage point of the "eye" symbol in the previous figure.

10. Crimp the hind legs forward. Rabbit-ear the front legs. Squash the ear. Repeat all three on the other side.

11. Reverse-fold the tail upwards (step 12 shows how far). Sink the middle of the back. Crimp the feet forward. Out-side-reverse-fold the front legs to make paws, and fold their tips back inside themselves to blunt them. Sink the corners of the ears to round them, and crimp the nose downwards.

12. Enlarged view. Narrow the tail with the long valley fold shown. Tuck the excess paper inside the model on the mountain fold shown. Crimp the nose, using two reverse folds.

13. Spread the layers of the ears (repeat behind). Blunt the nose with a small reverse fold.

14. Outside-reverse-fold the tail and spread the layers of the tip of the tail.

15. Finished Gerbil.

Dragonfly

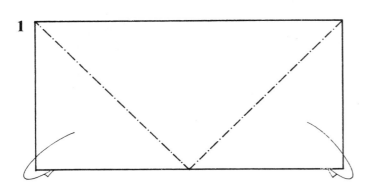

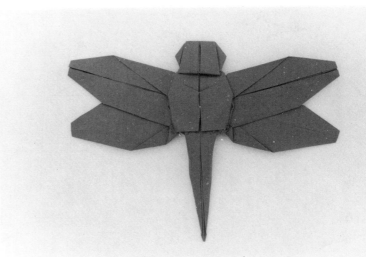

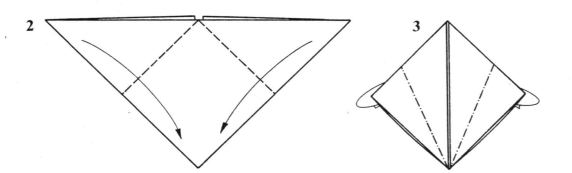

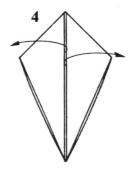

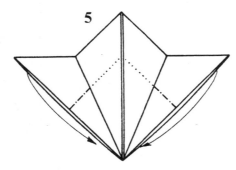

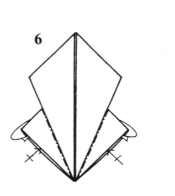

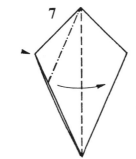

Paper: Use a 1:2 rectangle, white side up.
1. Mountain-fold the corners behind.
2. Valley-fold the corners down to the bottom.
3. Reverse-fold the corners into the interior of the model, along the angle bisectors.
4. Unfold the flaps covering the model, as if undoing an outside reverse fold.

5. Reverse-fold the outer points down to the bottom of the model.
6. Reverse-fold the four lower corners into the interior of the model. Turn the model over.
7. Spread-sink the left corner.

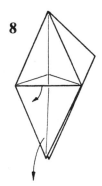

8

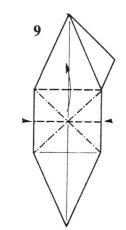

9

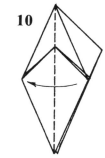

10

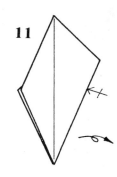

11

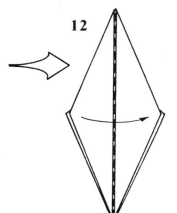

12

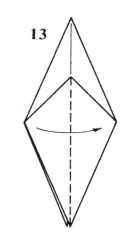

13

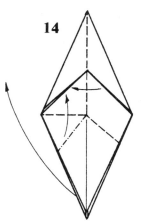

14

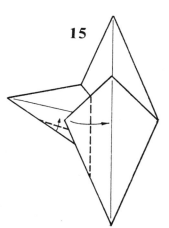

15

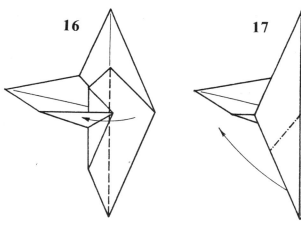

16

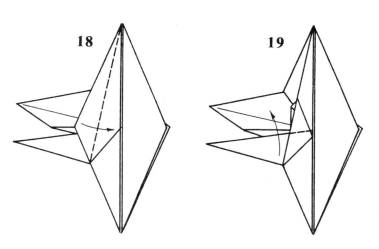

17

18

19

8. Grasp the top layer of paper at the bottom of the model and stretch it downward. The paper underneath the "hood" in the middle will come out.

9. Squeeze the side of the released paper at the indicated points and bring the middle of the small square back upwards, putting in the mountain folds as you go. Flatten the model out. You will have created a bird base out of half of the original rectangle.

10. Fold all the layers of the bird base back over to the left.

11. Repeat steps 7–10 on the right. Turn the model over.

12. Enlarged view. Book-fold one layer from left to right.

13. Book-fold one more layer.

14. Rabbit-ear the indicated flap upwards while bringing one layer over from the right. The point should poke out from the body at an angle slightly above the horizontal.

15. Swivel-fold. The corner extends slightly beyond the center line.

16. Book-fold one layer, right to left.

17. Reverse-fold.

18. Valley-fold.

19. Valley-fold one layer of this flap upwards, so that it lies flat.

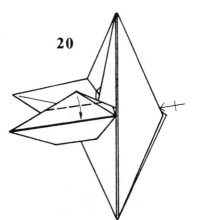

20

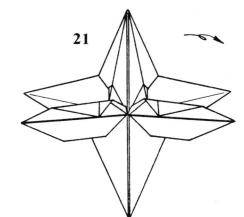

21

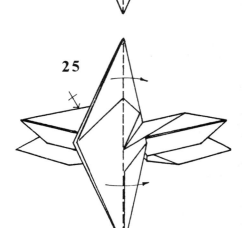

22

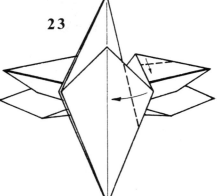

23

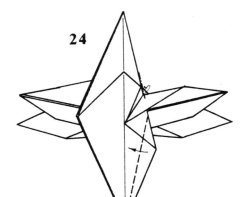

24

25

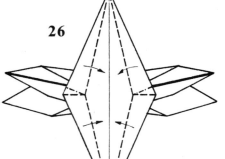

26

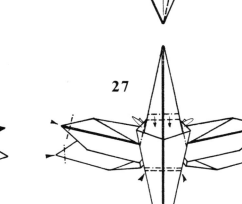

27

28

29

30

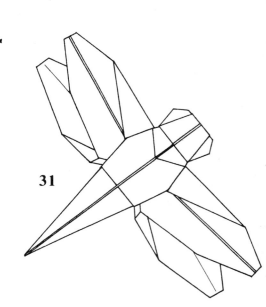

31

20. Valley-fold the corner back down. Repeat steps 12–20 on the right.

21. Like so. Turn the model over from side to side.

22. Book-fold one layer.

23. Swivel-fold.

24. Valley-fold the long, skinny edge. Mountain-fold the tiny region just above the wings into the interior of the model.

25. Book-fold one layer back to the right. Repeat steps 22–25 on the left.

26. Form two rabbit ears.

27. Fold the tiny flaps at the shoulders into the interior of the model. Pleat the head. Crimp the abdomen just below the wings. Sink the tips of all four wings.

28. Enlarged view of head. Pull out a single layer of paper from the bottom of each side of the head, as far as it will come.

29. Mountain-fold the tip of the head and the corners of the neck.

30. Reverse-fold the corners of the eyes.

31. Finished Dragonfly.

Bald Eagle

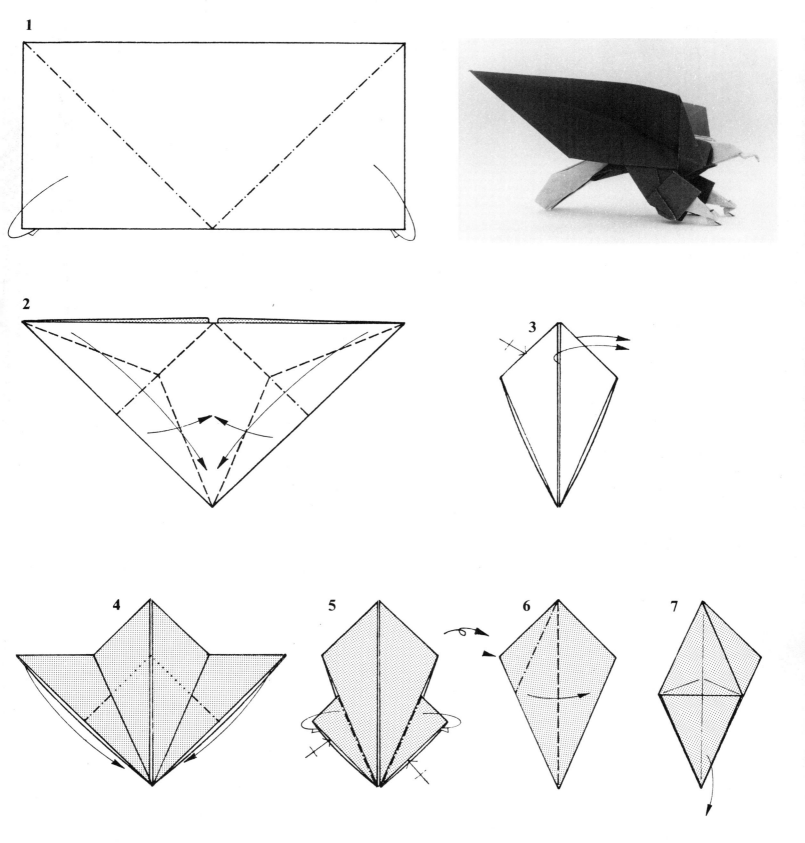

Paper: Use a 1:2 rectangle, white side up.
1. Mountain-fold two corners behind.
2. Rabbit-ear the corners.
3. Open out the two flaps shown.
4. Reverse-fold two corners down.

5. Reverse-fold four corners into the model. Turn the model over.
6. Spread-sink one layer.
7. Stretch one layer of paper as far as it will go.

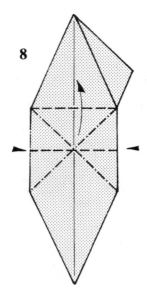

8

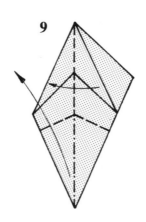

9

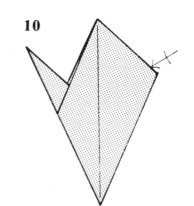

10

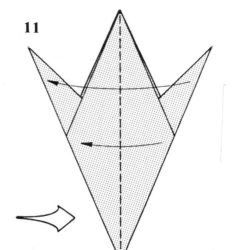

11

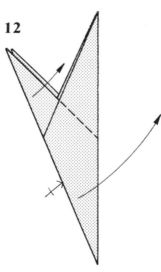

12

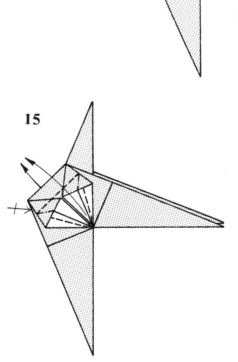

13

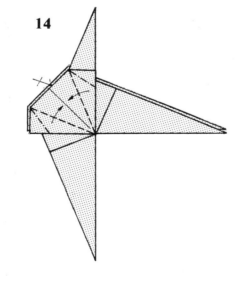

14

15

8. Reform the paper on the creases shown to make a bird base.

9. Reverse-fold one layer at the bottom while folding the bird base in half.

10. Repeat steps 6–9 on the right.

11. Enlarged view. Fold the entire model in half.

12. Open out the top layer of paper. Repeat behind.

13. Bring the tip of the upper left flap down to the junction of all the edges while opening out the edges of that flap. Repeat behind.

14. Squash-fold the edges shown. Repeat behind.

15. Petal-fold the tip as far as it will go. Repeat behind.

16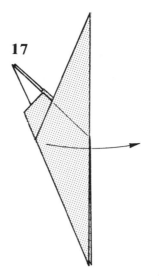

17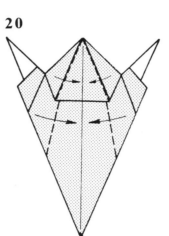

18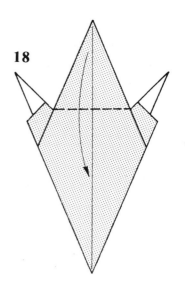

19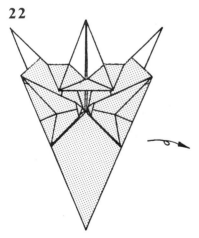

20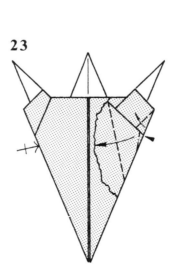

21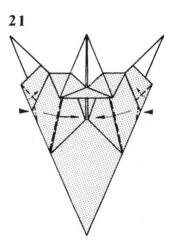

22

23

24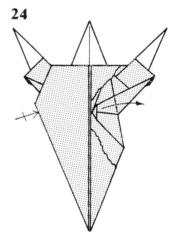

16. Fold the point in half, restoring the model to the configuration of step 12 (with the tip color-changed now). Repeat behind.

17. Open the model up again, vertically.

18. Fold the top point down as far as it will go.

19. Fold the tip back upwards, but spread the edges as shown.

20. Valley-fold edges as shown. The body folds extend up underneath the head.

21. Fold the next layer of the body in; the edges of the legs will swivel upwards and the corners will need to be slightly sunk (as in the Rocket).

22. Like so. Turn the paper over.

23. Cutaway view of the right side. Swivel the hidden layer of paper to match up with the layers underneath. Repeat on the left.

24. Without undoing the swivel fold, valley-fold the hidden layer back to the right. Repeat on the left.

25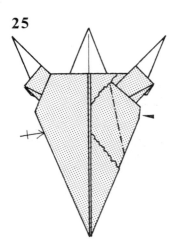

26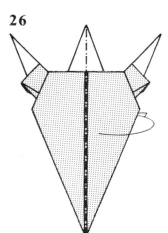

27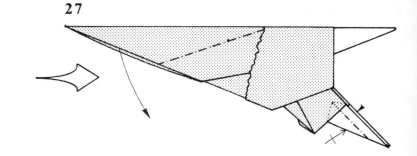

28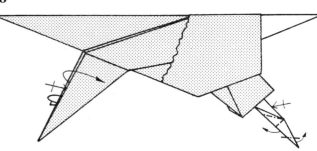

29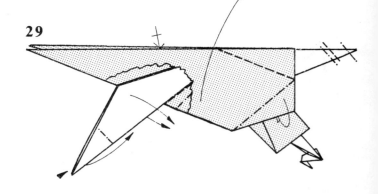

30

31

25. Again, without undoing the swivel, push the indicated corner inside itself (on the creases made in the previous steps). This is called a closed sink. It is so named because the point being sunk remains closed (in a normal, or open, sink the point gets opened out flat halfway through the sink). Repeat on the left.

26. Mountain-fold the model in half.

27. Enlarged view. Reverse-fold the tail (the left point) downward. Reverse-fold the leading edge of the leg on the mountain fold shown. The dotted lines show where additional folds inside the leg must be made to accommodate the mountain folds. Repeat on the other leg.

28. Wrap all possible layers from the inside of the tail around to the outside. Form feet with three reverse folds.

29. Sink the tip of the tail. Crimp the paper where the tail meets the body. Swivel-fold each wing upwards. Form a beak with a crimp (two parallel reverse folds) and another reverse fold for the tip.

30. Detail of foot. Pleat the leg so that it tips forward. Repeat behind.

31. Finished Bald Eagle.

Grasshopper

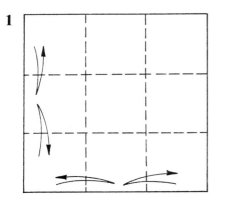

1

2

3

4

5

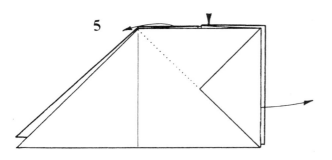

6

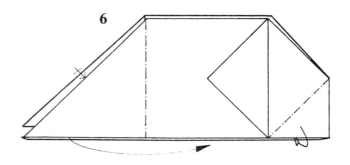

Paper: Use a square, white side up.

1. Crease the paper into thirds, both ways.

2. Mountain-fold two corners.

3. Fold a Waterbomb Base with the remaining square.

4. Enlarged view. Sink the top third of the Waterbomb Base. Valley-fold the two truncated corners of the shape to the left (front and rear).

5. There are two corners in the middle of the top edge of the model, resulting from the sink. Reverse-fold the left corner as far down as it will go. Simultaneously, sink the right corner down and pull the paper between the two rightward layers of the model out as far as it will go.

6. Like so. Reverse-fold the two left corners into the interior of the model. Reverse-fold the lower right corner of the model as well.

7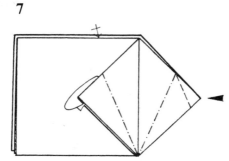

8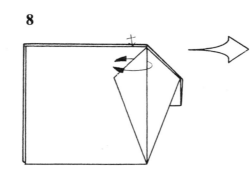

9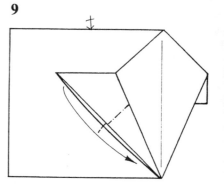

10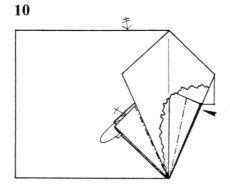

11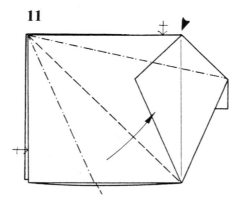

12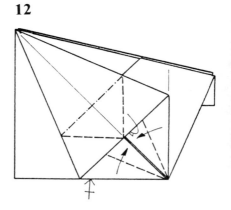

13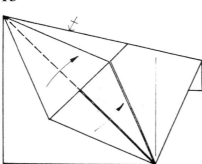

14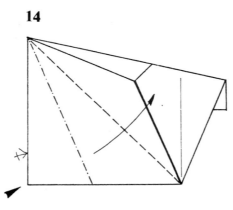

15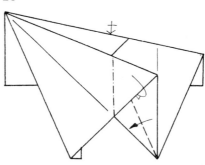

7. The right portion of the model now resembles a Preliminary Fold. Reverse-fold the left corner of that Preliminary Fold; repeat behind. Sink the corresponding right corner of the Preliminary Fold.

8. Unfold the indicated layer of paper. Repeat behind.

9. Enlarged view. Reverse-fold the corner down to the bottom of the model. Repeat behind.

10. Reverse-fold the corners shown—two in front, two in back. Sink the hidden point at the right.

11. Closed-sink the long, triangular region at the top of the model. Squash-fold the lower left corner symmetrically. Repeat behind.

12. Petal-fold the result of the previous step, but turn the point of the petal fold into the interior of the model. Repeat behind.

13. Valley-fold one layer. Repeat behind.

14. Squash-fold the remaining layer of paper. Repeat behind.

15. Reverse-fold as shown. Repeat behind.

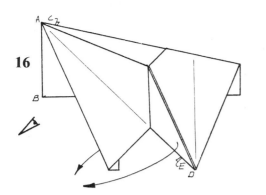

16

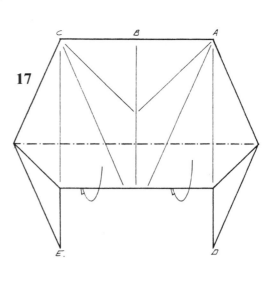

17

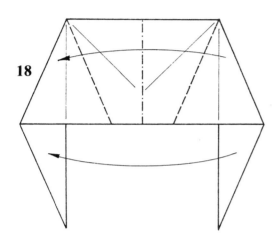

18

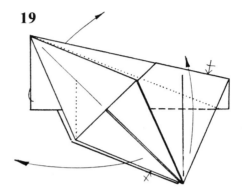

19

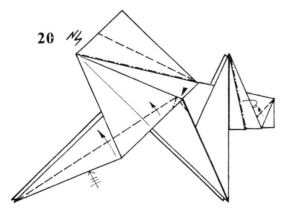

20

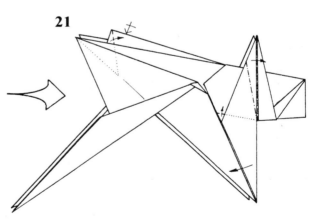

21

16. Note the labeling of points. Stretch points D and E apart. The result will not lie flat. The region bounded by A–E, however, will lie flat.

17. View from 16. Fold the long horizontal edge up inside the model.

18. Reform model on the creases shown. Flatten the model out.

19. Reverse-fold the middle layers of paper as far as they will go (along the dotted line). Reverse-fold the longest points at the bottom of the model (the soon-to-be back legs) as far as

they will go to the left (also along dotted lines). Valley-fold one layer upwards at the right.

20. Crimp the back. Valley-fold one layer of each back leg, forming a tiny spread-sink at the end of the valley fold. Repeat on the inside of each leg. Swivel-fold the leading edge of the vertical point at the right (the antenna). Repeat behind.

21. Enlarged view. Reverse-fold the layers of the tail that are almost hidden inside the body. Pivot the trailing edge of the antenna forward; one of the front legs will simultaneously swing down.

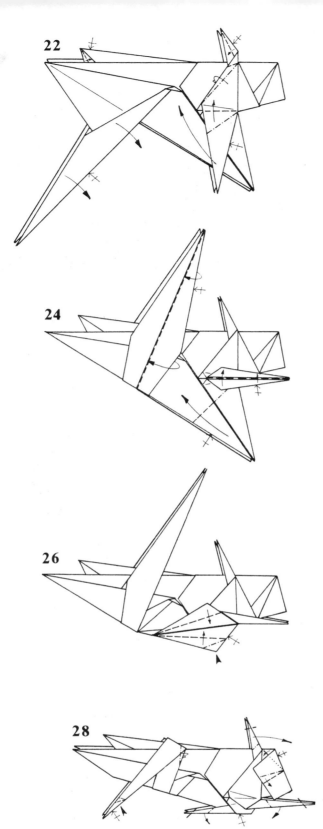

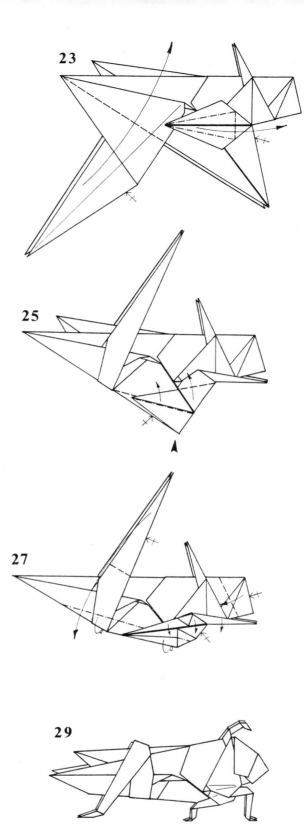

22. Unfold the top layer only of each back leg. Narrow the tail further. Narrow the antenna with another swivel fold. Squash-fold each front leg. Repeat behind.

23. Valley-fold the back leg assembly as far upwards as possible. Petal-fold the front leg forwards. Repeat behind.

24. Tuck the leading edge of each hind leg inside itself (this locks the leg into an upright position). Reverse-fold the remaining points at the bottom of the model upwards. They will become the middle legs. Valley-fold the front leg in half.

25. Reverse-fold the bottom of the middle leg. Open its top half upwards. Repeat behind.

26. Narrow the middle leg with valley folds and spread-sinks.

27. Narrow the underside of the body. Outside-reverse-fold the head. Valley-fold the rear legs downwards.

28. Crimp feet on the rear legs. Narrow the "knees" of the rear legs with mountain folds. Form front and middle legs and feet with reverse folds. Reverse-fold the antennae forward. Crimp the head, forming eyes.

29. Finished Grasshopper.

Dimetrodon

1

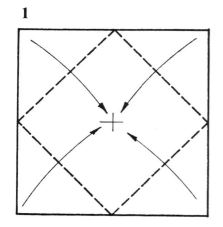

2

3

4

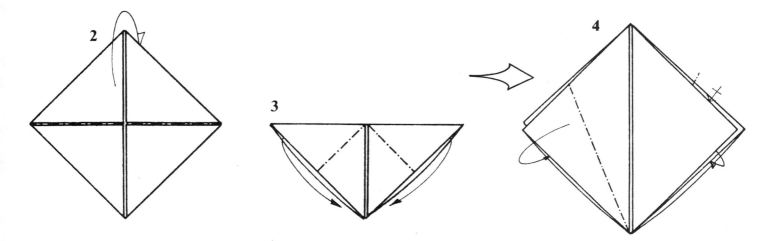

5

6

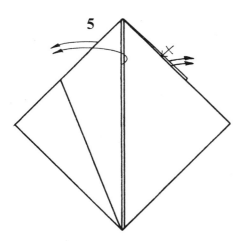

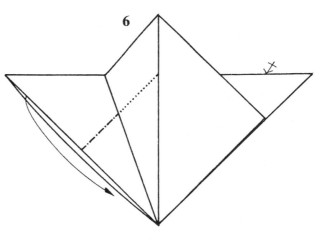

Paper: Use a square, white side up.
1. Fold the four corners to the center.
2. Mountain-fold in half along a diagonal.
3. Reverse-fold the corners to the bottom.
4. Enlarged view. Reverse-fold one corner on the left into the model. Repeat on the right, but on the rear layer.

5. Unfold the layer shown. Repeat on the right, behind.
6. Reverse-fold the corners shown down to the bottom of the model.

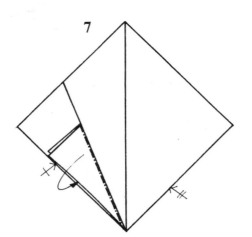

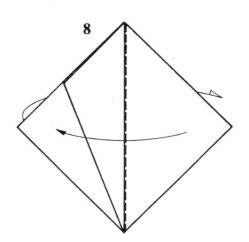

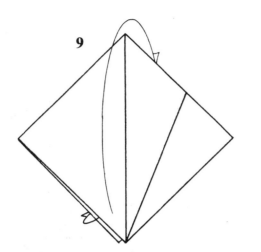

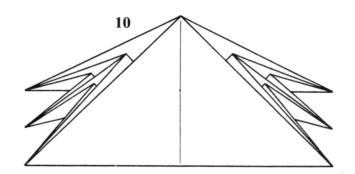

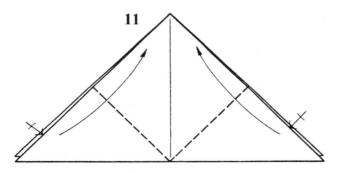

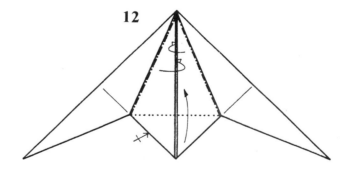

7. Reverse-fold four corners inside.

8. Book-fold one layer from right to left in front, and one layer from left to right behind.

9. Turn the model inside-out.

10. Like so. Flatten the model out.

11. Fold the four corners at the bottom of the model up to the top of the model.

12. Mountain-fold the central edges behind. The bottom middle point comes up in the process. Repeat behind.

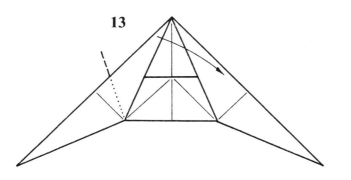

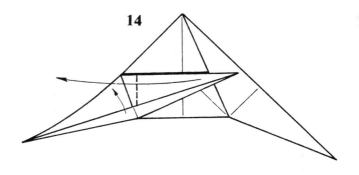

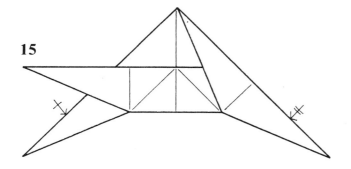

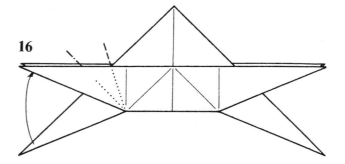

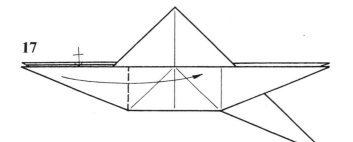

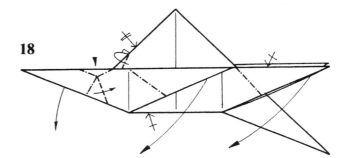

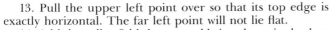

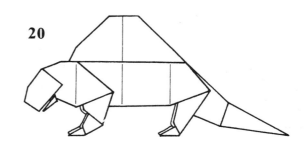

13. Pull the upper left point over so that its top edge is exactly horizontal. The far left point will not lie flat.

14. Add the valley fold shown, and bring the point back to the left. Now, flatten everything out.

15. Like so. Repeat on the right side, and behind.

16. Crimp the lower left point upwards so that it lines up with the other two points.

17. Swing one layer from left to right. Repeat behind.

18. Crimp the head (the left point) downwards, sinking the top of it as you do. Mountain-fold the edges of the sail where it joins the body. Reverse-fold all four legs downward.

19. Sink the tip of the sail (ideally, this should be a closed sink, but a normal sink will do). Reverse-fold the front of the head to form a mouth. Crimp the legs and tail. Repeat behind.

20. Finished Dimetrodon.

Deer

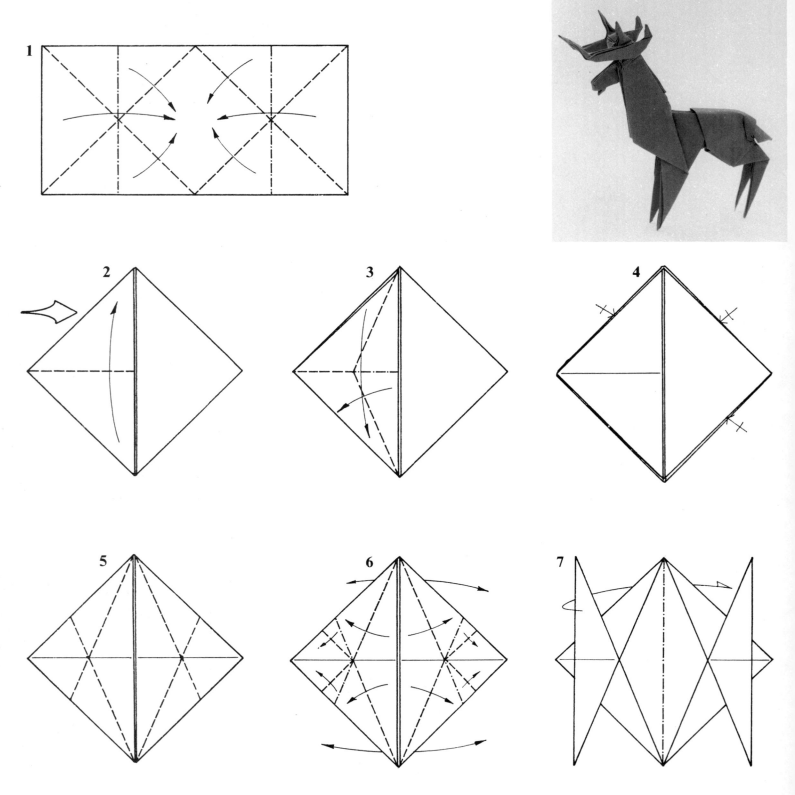

Paper: Use a 1:2 rectangle of thin paper, colored side up.
1. Fold a Waterbomb Base at each end of the rectangle.
2. Enlarged view. Lift one point up to the top.
3. Form a rabbit ear with a single layer of paper and bring the rest of the point back down.
4. Repeat on the other three points.
5. Add the angle bisector creases.
6. Form mountain and valley folds as shown. The raw edges of the paper that are in the middle of the model move outwards.
7. Like so. Mountain-fold in half.

8

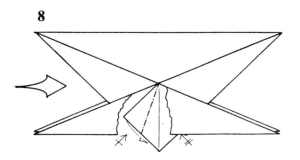

9

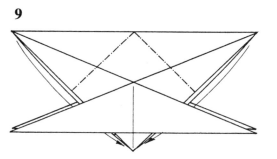

10

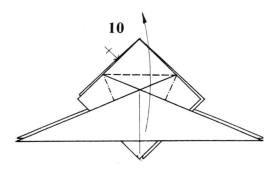

11

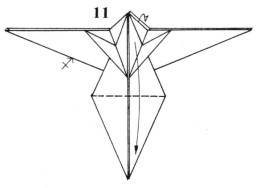

12

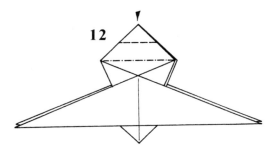

13

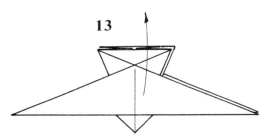

14

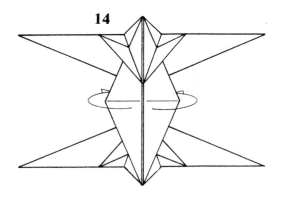

15

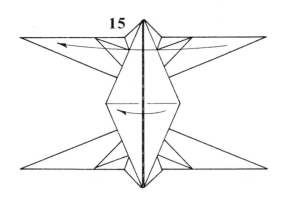

8. Enlarged view. Reverse-fold the hidden corners as shown, in four places.

9. Reverse-fold the corners down to the base of the model.

10. Petal-fold. It will be necessary to form a set of gussets (shown in the next drawing).

11. Valley-fold, front and rear.

12. Double-sink the point shown.

13. Lift one layer up.

14. Wrap the indicated layers of paper from front to back.

15. Fold one layer over to the left.

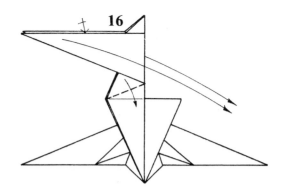

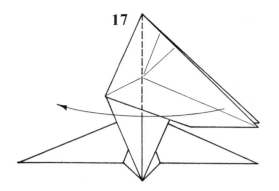

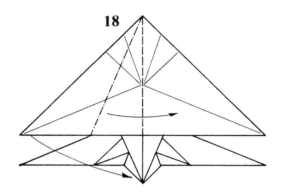

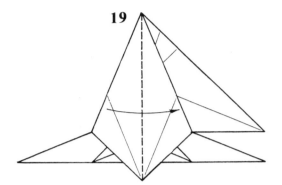

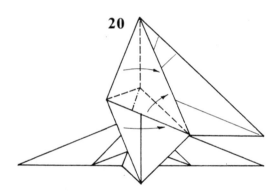

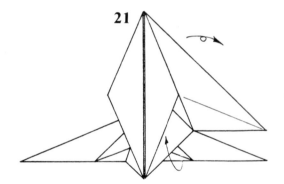

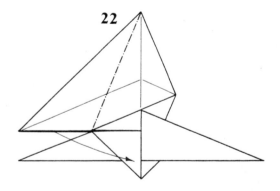

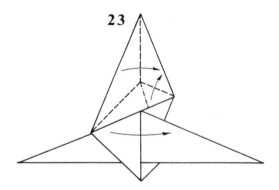

16. Bring the two long points down to the lower right. In the process, several folds will come undone.

17. Valley-fold one layer back to the left.

18. Squash-fold symmetrically.

19. Valley-fold.

20. Fold one more layer over to the right, incorporating the rabbit ear into the triangular region of paper.

21. Bring the long horizontal point at the lower right in front of the vertical point in the center of the bottom. Turn the model over.

22. Reverse-fold the remaining point down to the bottom of the model.

23. Fold one layer back to the right, incorporating the rabbit ear as shown.

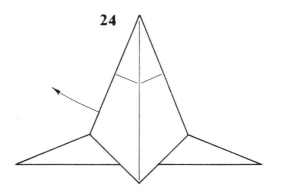

24

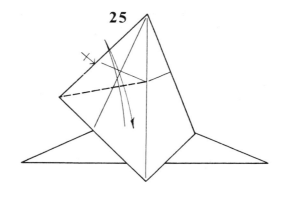

25

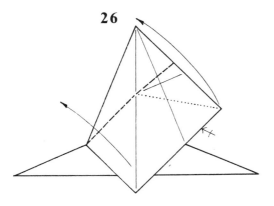

26

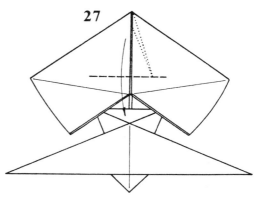

27

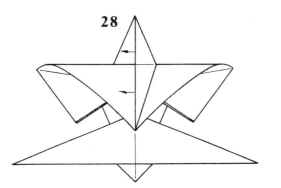

28

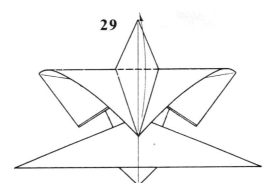

29

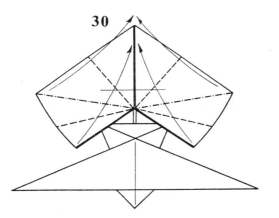

30

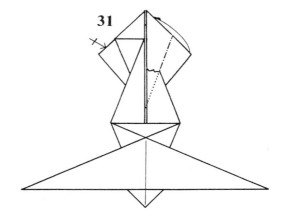

31

24. Pull out the hidden layer immediately under the flap on the left.

25. Crease this blunt flap from its corner to the intersection of the old creases shown. When that is done, fold the flap over to the right and do the same thing on the right.

26. Bring the corner of the blunt flap up so that it lies directly above the center line. The lower portion of the valley fold lies on existing creases, as does the fold indicated by the hidden line. The model will not lie flat.

27. The result looks like this, with the lower corners poking up in the air. Petal-fold the top corner; however, crease the valley-fold only as far as is necessary to make the petal fold.

28. Pull the paper out from under the petal fold to make it symmetric.

29. Fold the point back up to the top of the model.

30. Form a distorted Preliminary Fold.

31. Reverse-fold the edges in to lie along the center line.

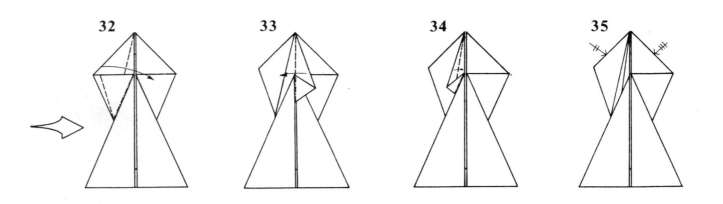

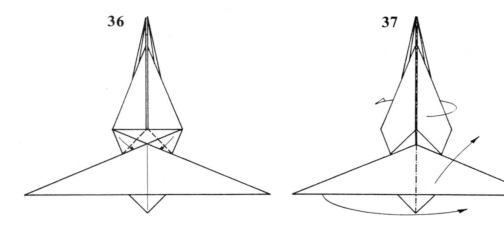

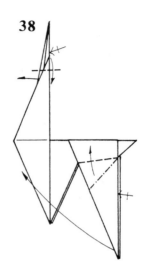

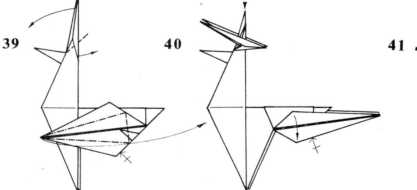

32. Enlarged view of head. Reverse-fold the edge over to the right . . .

33. . . . and back . . .

34. . . . and over again.

35. Repeat two more times on the left, and three times on the right.

36. Tuck the corners shown inside the long, horizontal triangle.

37. Mountain-fold the vertical portion of the model in half and swing the bottom over to the right.

38. Valley-fold the outermost tines of the antlers down. Reverse-fold the head out from the interior of the model. Squash-fold the hind legs. Repeat behind.

39. Pivot the antlers down—the long portion comes to the left, while the short tine goes to the right. Petal-fold the hind leg. Repeat behind.

40. Sink the long central point in the antlers down into the head. Valley-fold the hind leg in half. Repeat behind.

41. Reverse-fold the nose back and forth to make a mouth. Reverse-fold the fore and aft tines of the antlers, and pinch the center tines. Crimp the front legs. Reverse-fold the back legs. Repeat behind. Crimp the tail down.

42. Finished Deer.

Pegasus

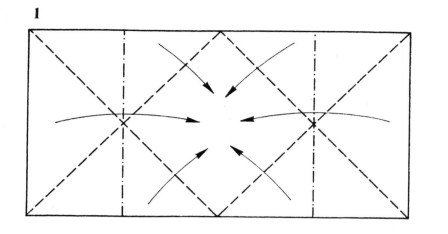

1

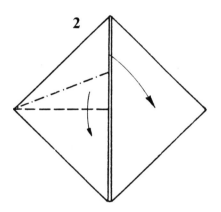

2

3

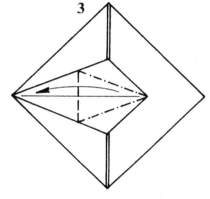

4

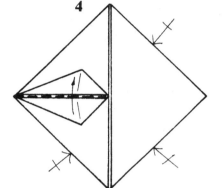

5

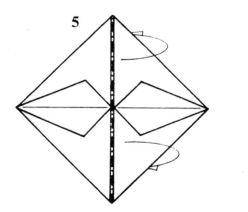

6

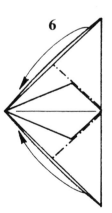

7

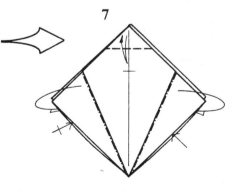

Paper: Use a 1:2 rectangle of thin paper, white side up.
1. Fold a Waterbomb Base on each half of the rectangle.
2. Squash-fold one point symmetrically.
3. Petal-fold.
4. Fold the point in half. Repeat on the other three points.

5. Mountain-fold the paper in half.
6. Reverse-fold the corners over to the left side.
7. Enlarged view. Valley-fold the top corner down. Crease heavily, and unfold. Reverse-fold the four side corners in.

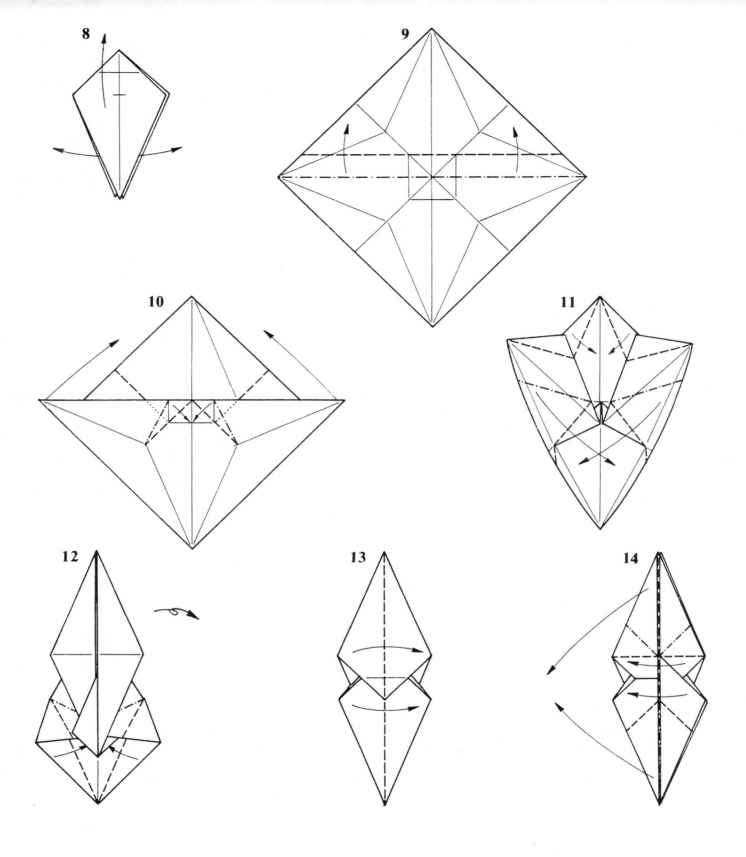

8. Open out the Bird Base to a square.

9. Form the valley and mountain folds based on the existing crease pattern.

10. Crimp the central region of the model. When you form the valley folds on the rear layer (which lie on existing creases) the portions of the valley fold of step 9 that lie near the edge come unfolded. The model will not lie completely flat.

11. Bring the two side corners back down to the bottom.

The valley folds at the top lie on existing creases, while the mountain folds in the middle fall where they must to flatten the model out.

12. The model is now flat. Reverse-fold the indicated layers inward. Turn the model over from side to side.

13. Valley-fold one layer of both the top and bottom portions.

14. Fold the layers back, but reverse-fold two points outward while doing so.

15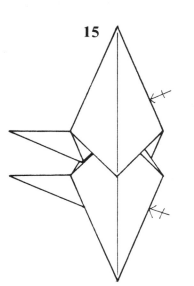

16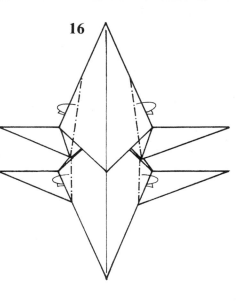

17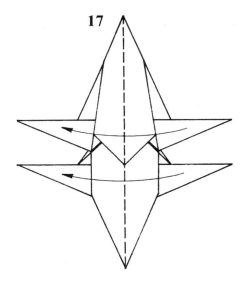

18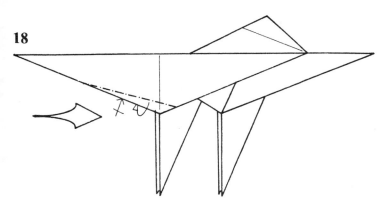

19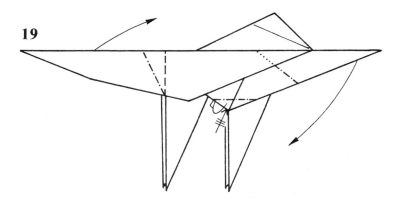

20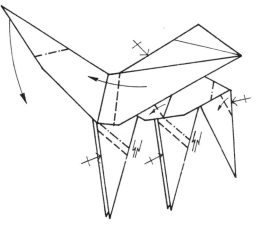

21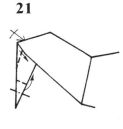

22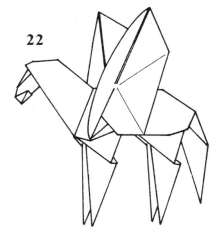

15. Repeat steps 13–14 on the right side of the model.

16. Mountain-fold the flaps shown into the interior of the model.

17. Fold the model in half.

18. Enlarged view. Mountain-fold the top layer underneath. Repeat behind.

19. Crimp the head upwards. Reverse-fold the tail downwards. Mountain-fold the corners above the rear legs inside the model. Repeat behind.

20. Reverse-fold the head downwards. Crimp all four legs. Reverse-fold the corners of the tail inward. Valley-fold the leading edge of each wing forward, so that the wings stand out from the body.

21. Reverse-fold the top edges of the head in to form ears and shape the head. Double-reverse-fold the tip to form a mouth.

22. Finished Pegasus.

CHAPTER 4

Three-Dimensional Folds

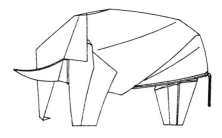

Three-dimensional folds pose a special challenge to the folder. By now, you have probably become used to using a hard folding surface to work on, flattening out the model after every step. Now, you will have to do some folding in mid-air. Most of the designs that follow let you do most of the folding on a flat model; then the fold is inflated, or otherwise "fluffed out," in the last few steps. This practice eases the burden of keeping edges straight and accurate. Also, the folds are no longer all at 180 degrees. You will be folding flaps at right angles to the plane of the paper, and sometimes gently curving the paper in lieu of making a sharp crease. Where necessary—particularly on the last step of the fold—I have included multiple views of a three-dimensional model. A symbol that will appear more and more often is the "eye" (◁), which is used when the paper is to be rotated out of the plane of the page. For example, if the "eye" is below the drawing, the next view will be of the underside of the model.

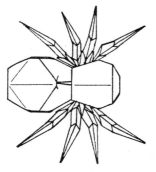

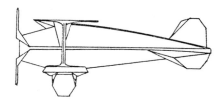

Cube

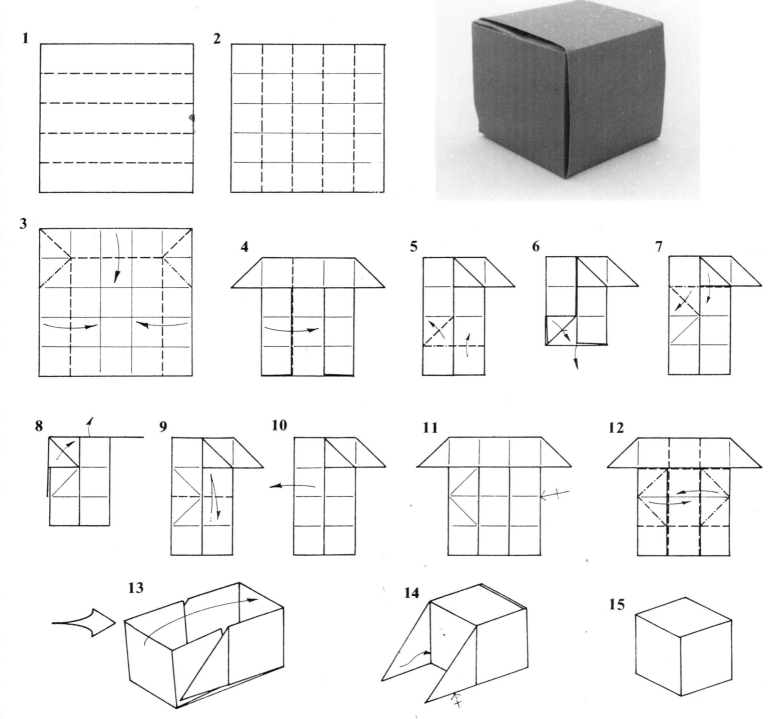

Paper: Use a square, white side up.

1. Valley-fold the paper into fifths vertically.

2. Valley-fold the paper into fifths horizontally.

3. Fold the top and sides into the center; make rabbit ears of the corners.

4. Fold the left edge over.

5. Lift up all the layers of the bottom edge of the model at right angles to the rest of the paper (so that it pokes up out of the page). Form the diagonal valley fold with the upper layers.

6. Undo step 5 and flatten the paper out.

7. Perform the same sequence as step 5 on the upper edge of the paper.

8. Crease and unfold.

9. Crease the model in half and unfold.

10. Return the model to the configuration of step 4.

11. Repeat steps 5–10 on the right.

12. Bring the centers of the sides in so that the top and bottom edges lift up (all this is done on the creases made in steps 4–11). Make sure that the triangular flaps at the top go outside of everything else.

13. Enlarged view. Rotate the box-like shape on the left inside the right half.

14. Tuck the triangular flaps into the pockets shown. Tweezers help at this point.

15. Finished Cube.

57

Stellated Cubocta

1

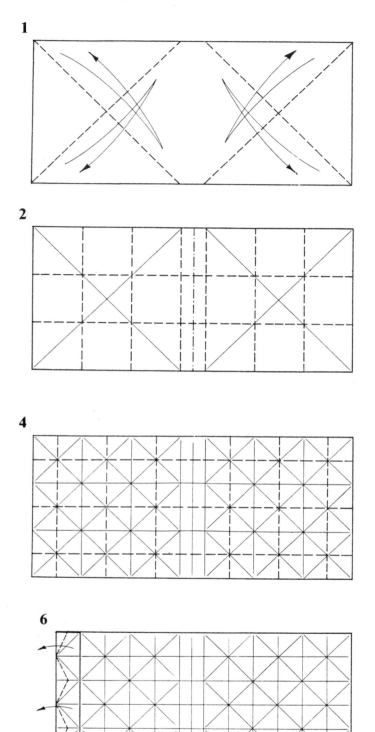

2

3

4

5

6

7

Paper: Use a 1:2.138 rectangle of foil-backed paper, white side up.

1. Crease the four corner diagonals.

2. Divide the rectangle into thirds along the short dimension. Crease valley folds through the intersections of the diagonals and the horizontal creases. Crease the mountain fold at the halfway point.

3. Add the valley folds shown.

4. Add more vertical and horizontal creases.

5. Fold the left edge over on an existing crease.

6. Crease the angle bisectors through both layers of paper. Unfold the flap.

7. This shows the crease pattern resulting from step 6. Repeat steps 5 and 6 on each of the vertical creases indicated by a repeat arrow.

8

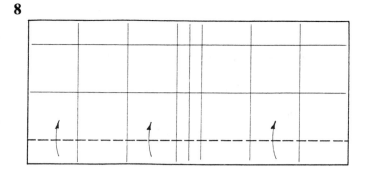

9

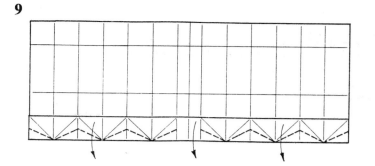

10

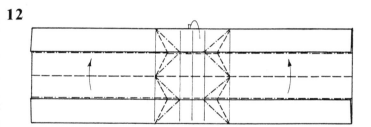

11

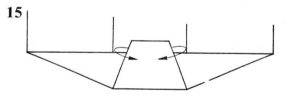

12

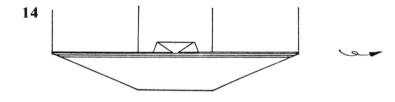

13

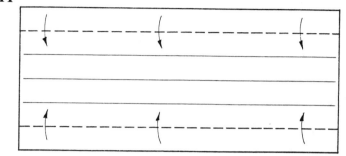

14

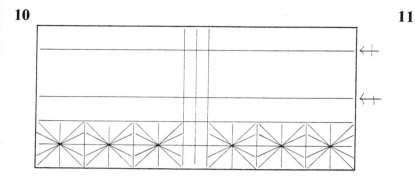

15

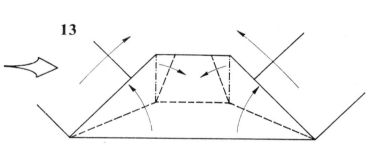

16

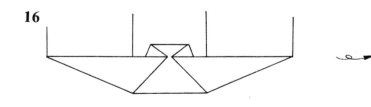

17

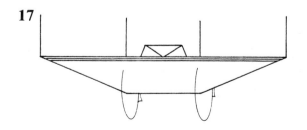

8. Fold the bottom edge up on an existing crease.

9. Crease the angle bisectors through both layers of paper. Unfold.

10. Repeat steps 8 and 9 on each of the two indicated creases.

11. Fold two edges in on existing creases.

12. Pleat the strip, incorporating the crimps shown on existing creases.

13. Enlarged view. Form two rabbit ears, folding all the layers of paper together as one.

14. Like so. Turn the model over.

15. Wrap one layer around to the front on the left and right.

16. Turn the model back over.

17. Wrap one layer behind.

18

19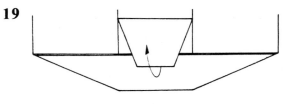

20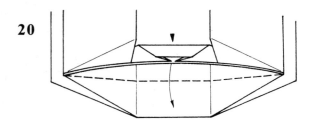

21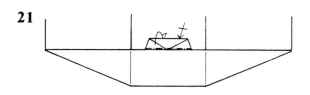

22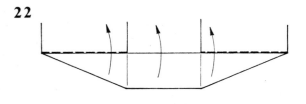

23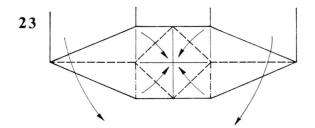

24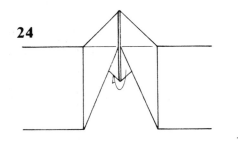

25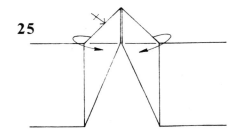

26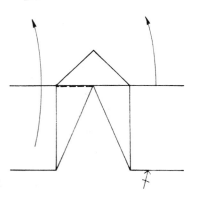

27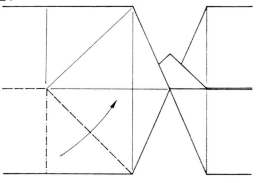

18. Pivot the layers inside the boat-like structure upward on the mountain folds shown.

19. Lift up the top layer slightly.

20. Closed-sink the edge shown as far downward as possible.

21. Mountain-fold the small flaps flush with the "gunwales" of the boat-like shape.

22. Lift up one layer.

23. Form two rabbit ears with all layers.

24. Fold the lower point behind and upward.

25. Wrap one layer from the middle around in front. Repeat behind.

26. Lift up one layer in front on the left and one in back on the right. From here through step 36, anything done on the front of the left side should be done on the back of the right side, and anything done on the front of the right should likewise be done on the back of the left.

27. Lift up one layer slightly.

28

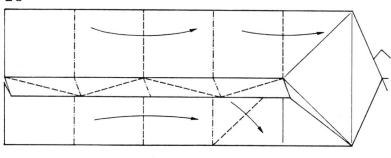

29

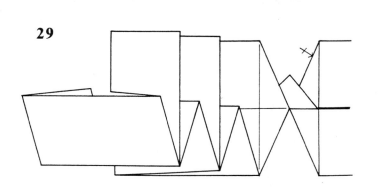

30

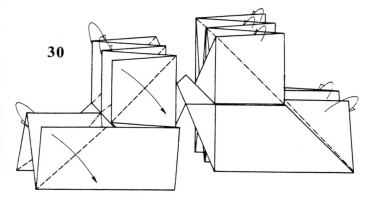

31

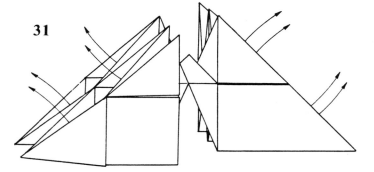

32

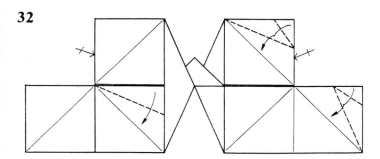

33

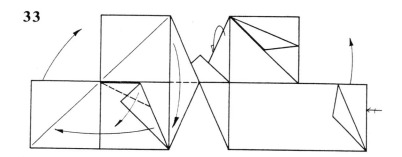

34

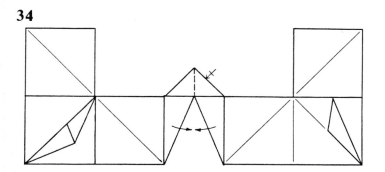

35

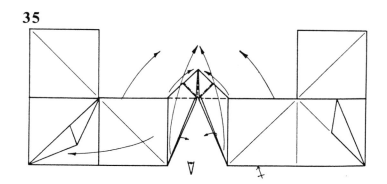

28. Collapse the long strip along the folds shown.

29. Like so. Flatten out and repeat on the right.

30. Valley-fold two flaps on the left and reverse-fold three edges on the right. Repeat on the other side of the model.

31. Pull out the layers that lie between the reverse folds of step 30. Repeat on the right.

32. Valley-fold the flaps as shown. Repeat behind.

33. Bring the top of the backwards-L-shape downward and pivot it 90 degrees clockwise. Repeat on the right.

34. Bring the edges shown together in front and back. They will be poking directly out of the paper.

35. Form a Preliminary Fold with the central region. There are three edges emanating from the junction on both the right and left sides. Spread those edges apart.

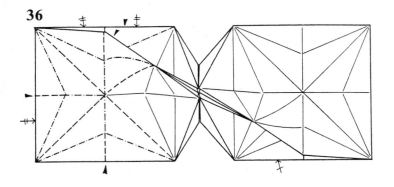

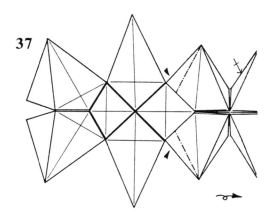

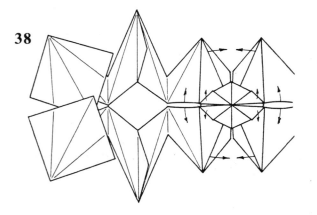

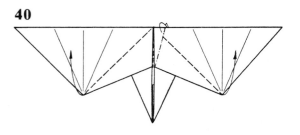

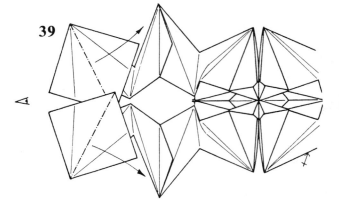

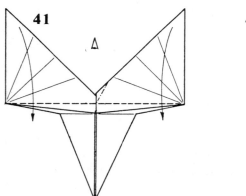

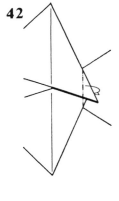

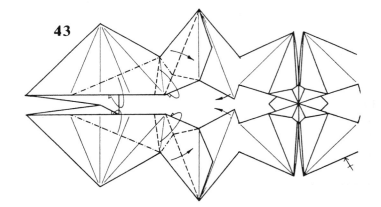

36. View from 35. Of the aforementioned three edges, two point toward the top of the page, two toward the bottom and two straight out. There are four edges shown on the left to be sunk on existing creases. There are six more in hidden layers that must be sunk similarly, and ten on the right side, making a total of twenty such sinks.

37. Sink the remaining two edges. This step must be performed at the same time as step 38, which is done on the underside of the fold. Again, the sinks are on existing creases and should be repeated on the right. Turn the model over.

38. Bring the tips of the central points together and spread the central layers apart. This will enable step 37 to be completed.

39. Lift the corners of the square flaps upwards.

40. View from 39. Make sure that the sides of the point at the bottom are pushed together; then tuck the center section over and lift up the outer corners.

41. Fold the triangular flaps downward.

42. View from 41, showing the locking fold. Mountain-fold this corner into the interior to lock the end together.

43. Bring the edges of the long points at top and bottom together. Mountain-fold the inside edges underneath to lock it. Repeat steps 39–43 on the right.

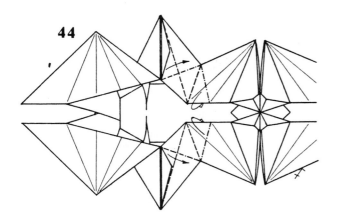

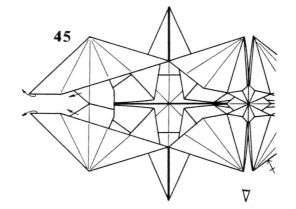

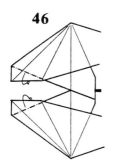

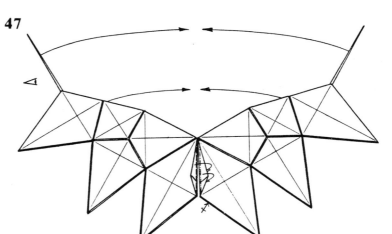

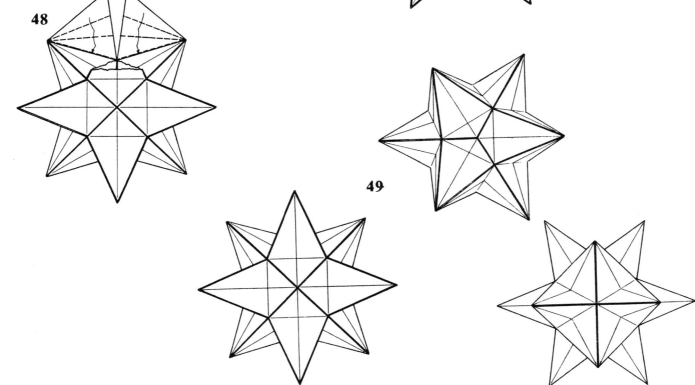

44. Lock the other edge of the long points similarly. Repeat on the right.

45. Pull out the excess paper on the underside of the flaps at the extreme left. Repeat on the right.

46. Fold the corners inside.

47. View from 45. Tuck both of the flaps at the bottom into one of the pockets next to them. Repeat behind. Bring the right and left halves of the model together.

48. View from 47. Fold each pair of flaps as one, over and over and down into the inside of the model. Push the model into a symmetric shape. There are fourteen points total, six four-sided points and eight three-sided points.

49. Finished Stellated Cubocta.

Rabbit

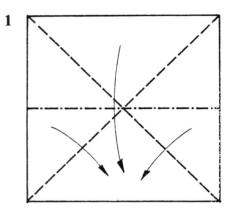

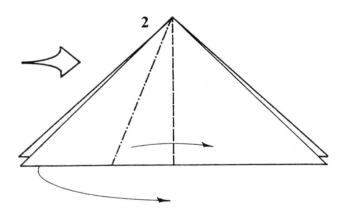

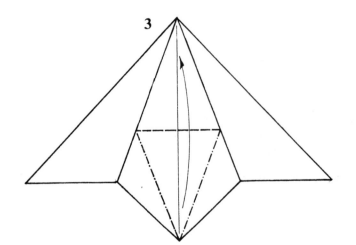

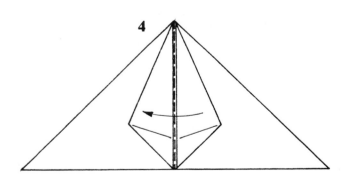

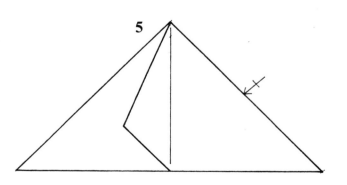

Paper: Use a square, white side up.
1. Fold a Waterbomb Base.
2. Enlarged view. Squash-fold the left flap.

3. Petal fold.
4. Fold the flap in half.
5. Repeat steps 2–4 on the right.

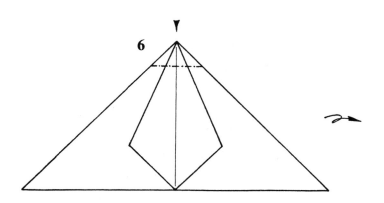

6

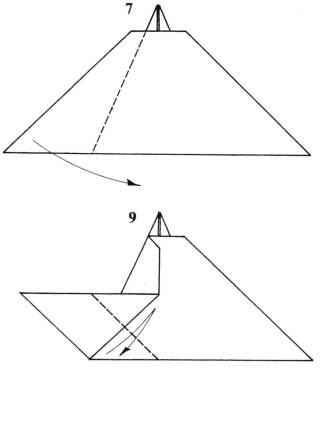

7

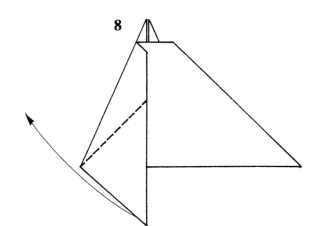

8

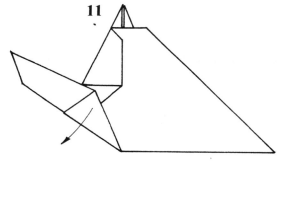

9

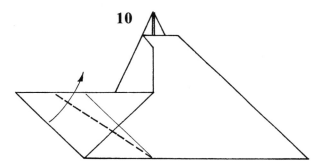

10

11

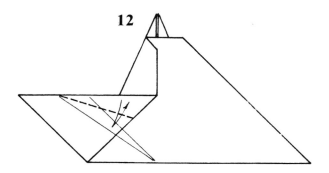

12

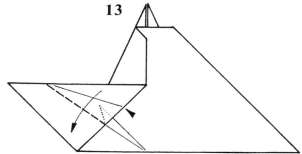

13

6. Sink one-sixth of the tip down into the model. The tips of the petal folds will be left sticking out. Turn the model over.

7. Valley-fold the left edge in to lie exactly vertical.

8. Valley-fold the flap out so that its upper edge is horizontal.

9. Fold the bottom left corner in to the center; crease and unfold.

10. Fold the edge back up at a lesser angle; the edge of the flap should intersect the edge of the rest of the model at the point shown in step 11.

11. Unfold.

12. Bisect the angle between the edge and the crease just made on the top layer of paper.

13. Valley-fold the upper portion of this flap on the existing crease and push in the edge where shown.

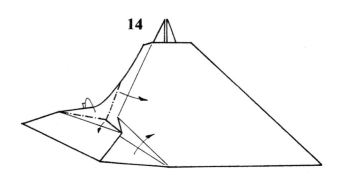

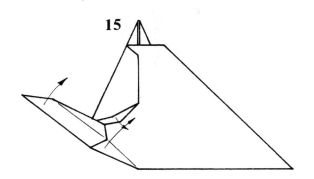

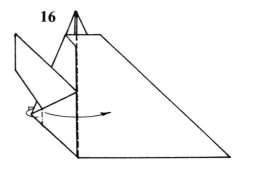

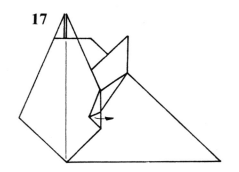

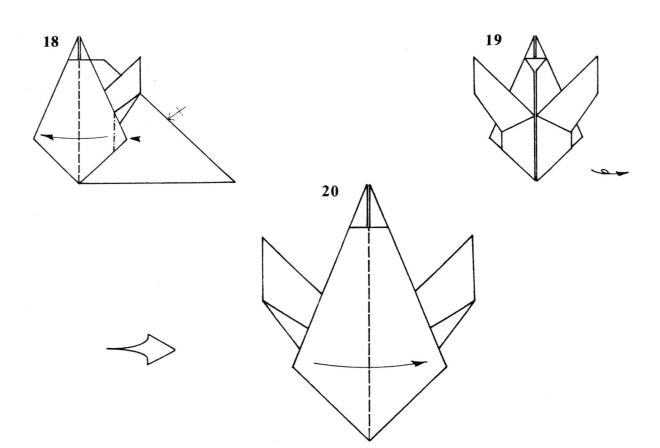

14. The flap is now poking up out of the paper. Bring the bottom edge in to the center and mountain-fold the top edge. The left half of the mountain fold lies on an existing crease.

15. Close up the flap, making new creases where necessary.

16. Fold the flap over to the right, and mountain-fold corner behind.

17. Unfold the corner.

18. Closed-sink the corner into the model. Fold one layer back to the left. Repeat steps 7–18 on the right.

19. The result. Turn the model over.

20. Enlarged view. Fold one layer over to the right.

21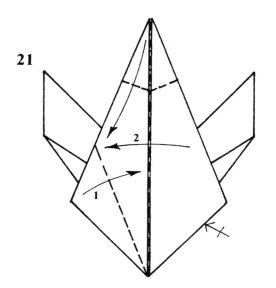

22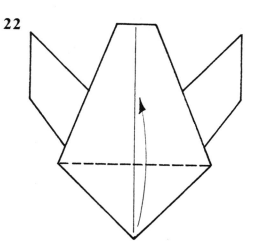

23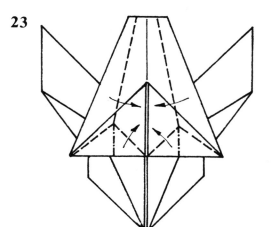

24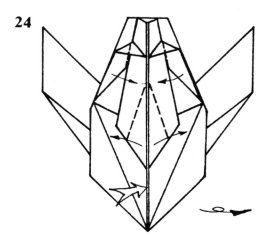

25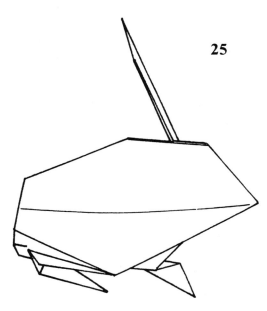

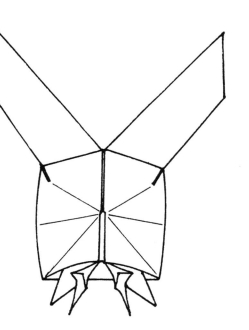

21. Valley-fold the lower left edge over to the center. Fold the right flap over the left one, reverse-folding the tip downward. Repeat steps 20 and 21 on the right side.

22. Valley-fold the bottom flap up as far as it will go.

23. Make two rabbit ears.

24. Fold the hind legs (at the top of the page) in toward the center. Bend the front legs outward. Inflate the model through the slit under the nose. Lift up the ears and turn the model over.

25. Finished Rabbit.

Elephant

1

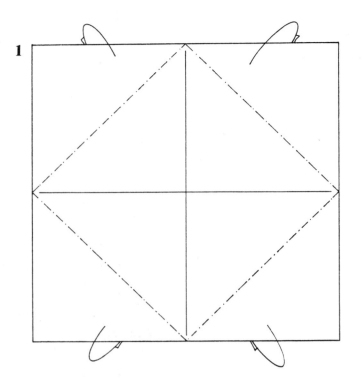

2

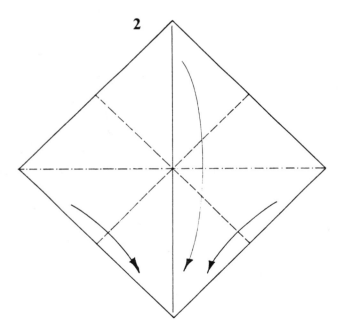

3

4

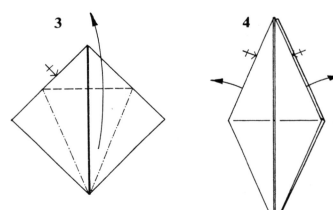

Paper: Use a square, white side up.
1. Valley-fold the paper in half vertically and horizontally, and fold the four corners behind to the center.

2. Make a Preliminary Fold from the remaining square.
3. Petal-fold, front and back.
4. Pull out the trapped layers of paper. Repeat behind.

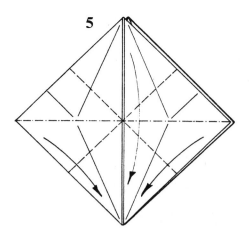

5

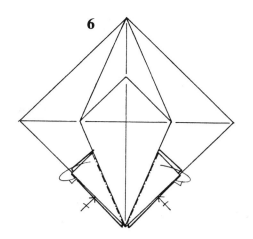

6

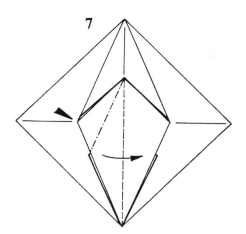

7

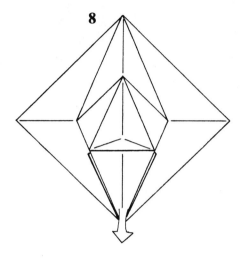

8

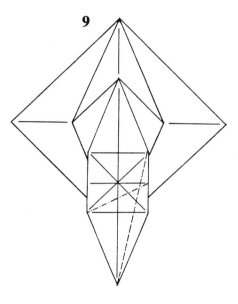

9

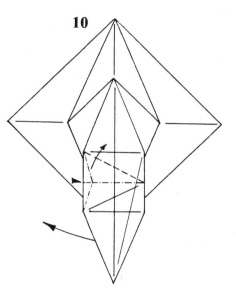

10

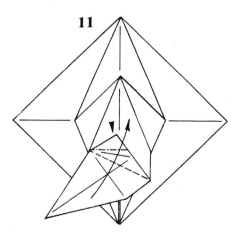

11

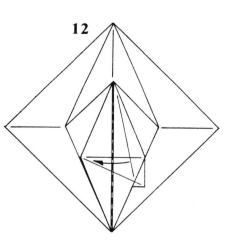

12

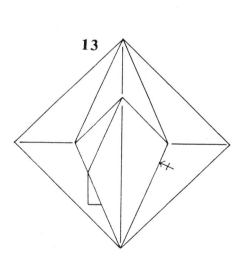

13

5. Form a Preliminary Fold with the released layers of paper on the front side only.

6. Reverse-fold four corners into the model.

7. Spread-sink symmetrically.

8. Stretch the point at the bottom and flatten out the paper.

9. Crease the angle bisector (the valley fold) and crease the mountain fold connecting the two points shown.

10. Crimp the upper layer of paper. It will be necessary to sink the left side and pivot the long point clockwise.

11. Sink the corner shown along a horizontal line. Valley-fold the long point upwards.

12. Book-fold one layer from right to left.

13. Repeat steps 7–12 on the right.

Elephant 69

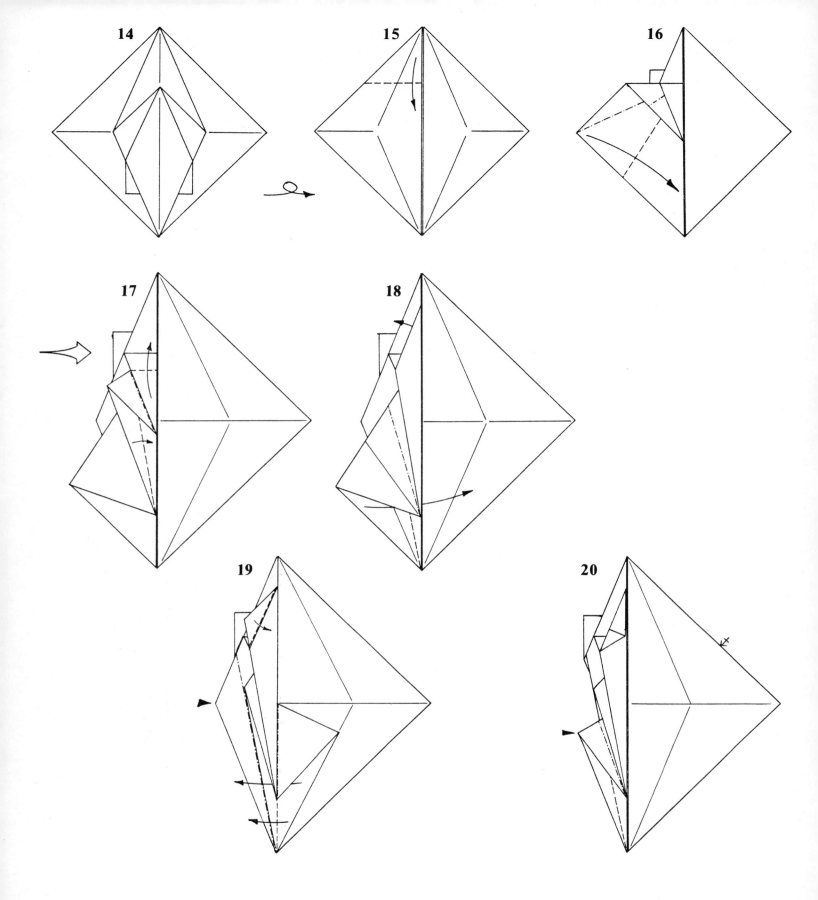

14. Turn the model over from top to bottom.
15. Fold one corner down as far as it will go.
16. Reverse-fold the corner down to lie on the center line.
17. Enlarged view. Petal-fold the top layer.
18. Pull out the hidden layer of paper at the top. Reverse-fold the long edge at the bottom to lie along the crease on the right side.

19. Wrap the layer at the top around. Reverse-fold the edge at the right over to the left. Closed-sink the left corner of the model. It is very important that this be a closed sink—that is, that the corner be inverted without coming unfolded. This locks the model together.
20. Reverse-fold the left edge in to the center. Repeat steps 15–20 on the right side.

21

22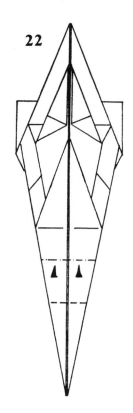

23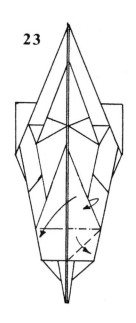

24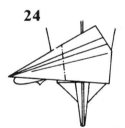

25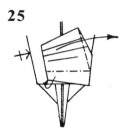

26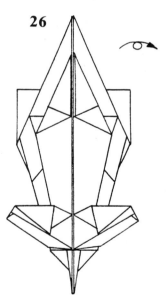

21. Valley-fold the hind legs (the two points at the bottom) upwards.

22. Crimp the tail up into the little pocket formed by the two closed sinks of step 19.

23. Squash-fold the hind leg on the right. The mountain fold shown should be at right angles to the edge, and the side not shown should be pulled up as far as it will go.

24. Mountain-fold (or sink, for added stability) the end of the hind leg (about half of its length).

25. Petal-fold the hind leg. Repeat steps 23–25 on the left.

26. Turn the model over.

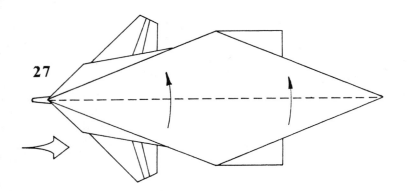

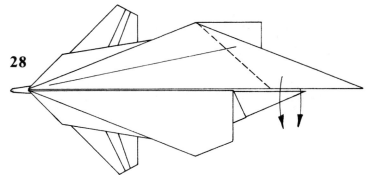

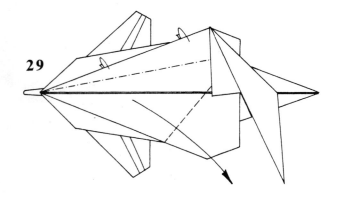

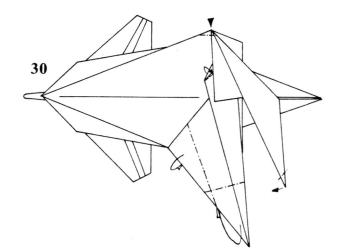

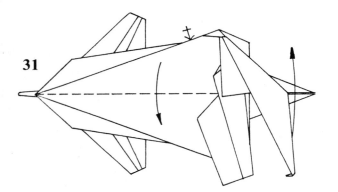

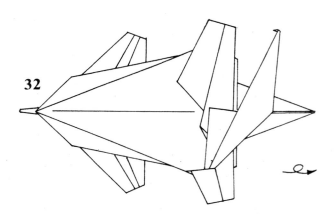

27. Enlarged view. Valley-fold one layer upward.

28. Outside-reverse-fold the trunk (the point on the right).

29. Fold the long point at the left downward, simultaneously forming a mountain fold on an existing crease. The leading edge of the result should be almost vertical.

30. Blunt the top corner with a closed sink. Reverse-fold the tiny corner under the ear. Shape the front leg with two mountain folds, and reverse-fold the tip of the trunk.

31. Rotate the trunk and body downward, and repeat steps 19–20 on the upper side of the model.

32. Turn the model over.

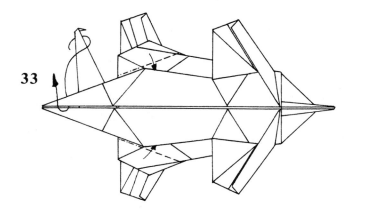

33

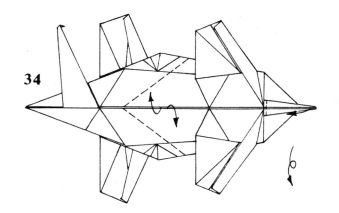

34

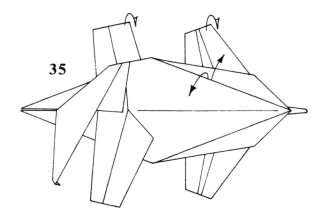

35

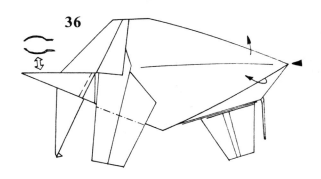

36

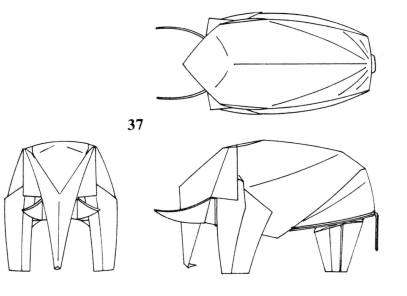

37

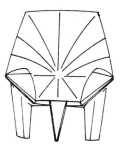

33. Thread the trunk between the tusks. Reverse-fold the indicated edges inside.

34. Crease the valley folds shown, and start to open out the model. Fold the tail down. Turn the model over.

35. Fold the right legs down and open out the back.

36. Curve the tusks and front legs. Partially sink the rear end so that it, too, opens out. Round the body.

37. Finished Elephant.

Parrot

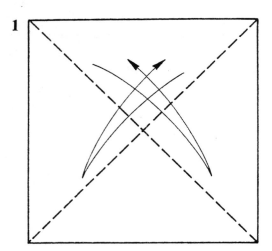

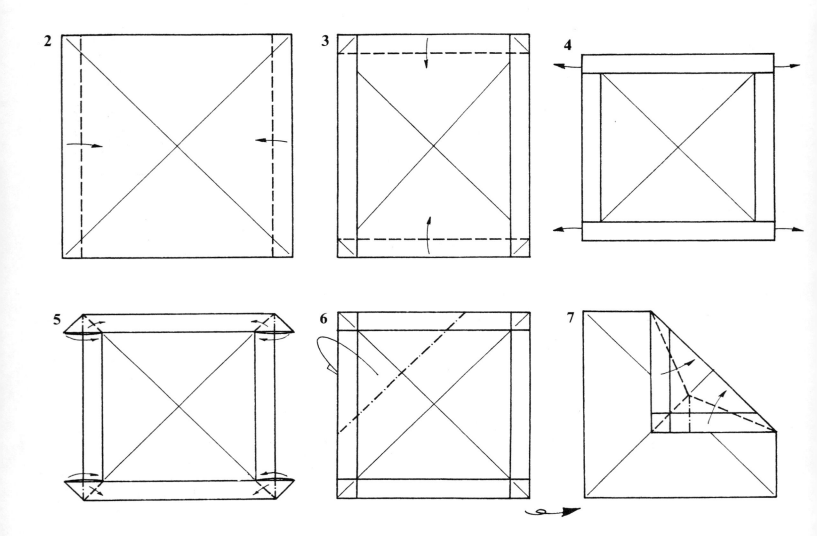

Paper: Use a square, colored side up.
1. Crease the diagonals.
2. Fold in one-twelfth of the width at each end.
3. Fold the same width over at the top and bottom.
4. Pull the corners out.

5. Squash-fold the four corners.
6. Fold one-third of the diagonal of the remaining square behind. Turn the model over.
7. Rabbit-ear the corner.

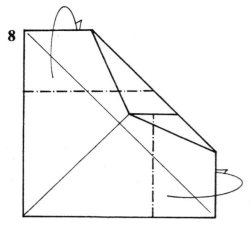

8

9

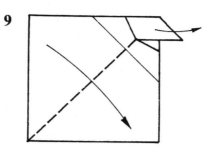

10

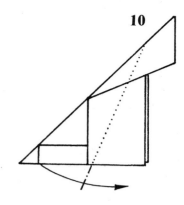

11

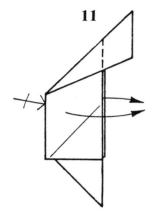

12

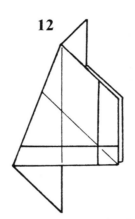

13

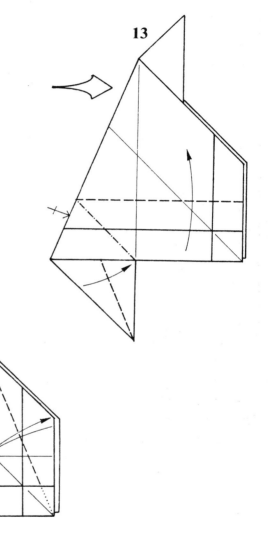

14

15

8. Fold the top and right edges behind.

9. Fold the model in half along the diagonal, pulling the rabbit ear out.

10. Reverse-fold the left corner so that the left edge is aligned with the right edges.

11. Fold the front and back edges over to the right.

12. Like so.

13. Enlarged view. Swivel-fold. The valley fold is exactly horizontal.

14. Fold the flap back down. Repeat behind.

15. Valley-fold the angle bisectors.

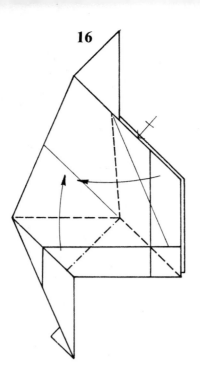

16

17

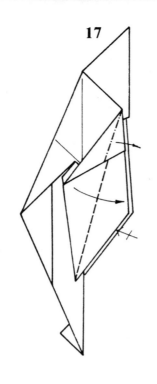

18

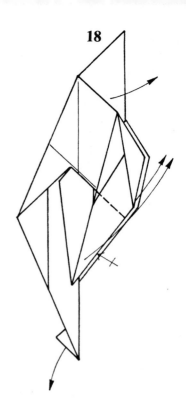

19

20

21

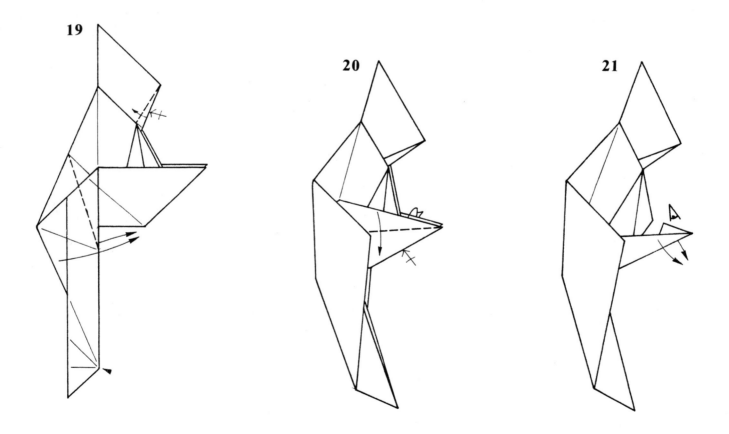

16. Fold a rabbit ear. The two lower valley folds lie on existing creases. The upper one connects the intersection of the lower two with the intersection of the edge and the crease made in step 15. Repeat behind.

17. Fold the left edge over along an existing crease. Pull the little hood at the upper end out. Repeat behind.

18. Valley-fold the feet upwards. Pull the head out so that the crease formed in the head in step 11 lines up with the edge of the body. Pull the extra paper in the tail as far out as possible.

19. Valley-fold the bottom edges of the head. Reverse-fold the tail where shown, making a closed sink at the corner of the tail.

20. Fold the top edge of the leg down along the angle bisector. Repeat behind.

21. Open the tip of the foot out flat.

22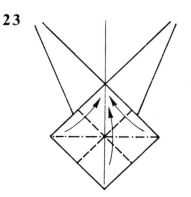

23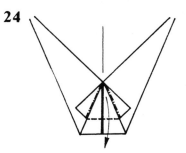

24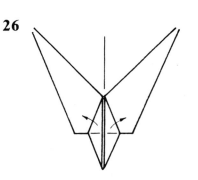

25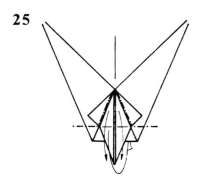

26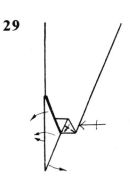

27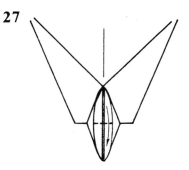

28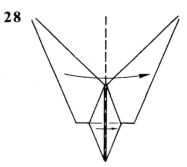

29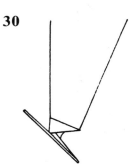

30

22. Enlarged view from 21. Mountain-fold the square in half, folding all layers as one. Unfold.

23. Form a Preliminary Fold.

24. Petal-fold.

25. Mountain-fold the bottom of the "Bird Base" to the rear. Petal-fold the two "legs" of the Bird Base.

26. Spread the layers of the petal fold.

27. Fold the single point inside the other layers downward. There should now be two points wrapped around, one pointing down, and one point behind, pointing up.

28. Fold the leg in half again.

29. Flatten out the foot.

30. Like so.

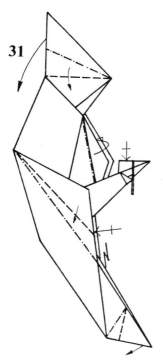
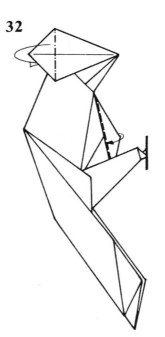
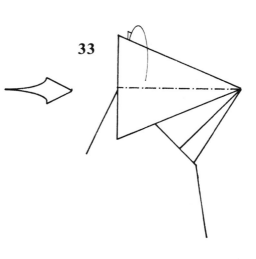
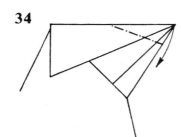
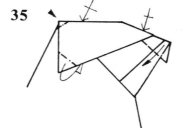
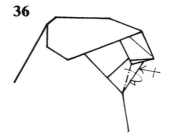
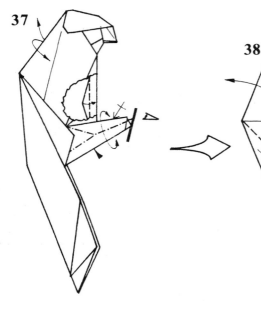
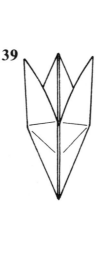
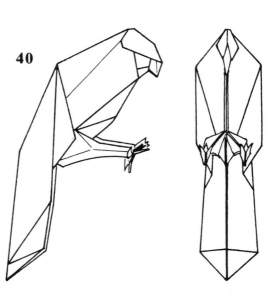

31. Repeat steps 21–30 on the other leg. Squash-fold the top of the head. Crimp the sides and tip of the tail. Repeat behind. Mountain-fold a single layer of the chest inside.

32. Mountain-fold the tip of the head inside.

33. Enlarged view. Mountain-fold the top of the head behind.

34. Reverse-fold the beak.

35. Mountain-fold the corners at the "cheeks." Sink the top of the head. Valley-fold the sides of the beak down.

36. Fold the edges underneath the beak inside.

37. Reach inside the body (from the bottom) with tweezers, and fold the blunt triangle over to lock the chest. Pinch the legs. Open out the back to make the model three-dimensional.

38. View from 37, enlarged. Pinch the trailing claw and spread the two front claws to expose the third one. Repeat on the other foot.

39. Like so.

40. Finished Parrot.

Biplane

1

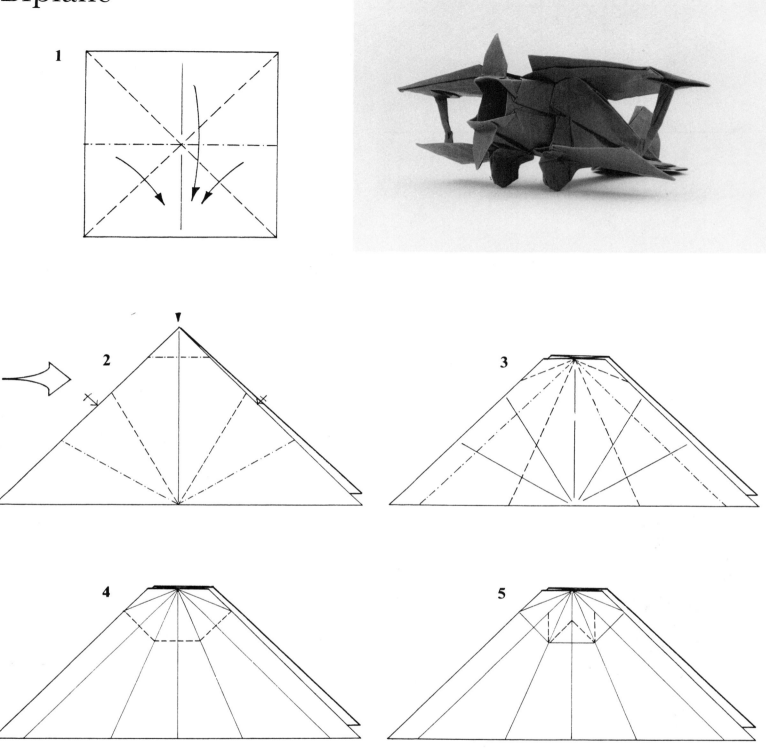

2

3

4

5

Paper: Use a square, white side up.

1. Fold a Waterbomb Base.

2. Sink one-sixth of the height down into the model. Pleat the front and back flaps with angle trisectors. Repeat behind.

3. Form the creases shown. The mountain folds run parallel to the outside edges, and the valley folds are angle bisectors.

4. Crease the valley folds shown. They are all perpendicular to the creases that bisect them.

5. Add four more creases. The two outside creases are exactly vertical, while the ones at 45 degrees, if extended, would connect up with the top corners of the paper.

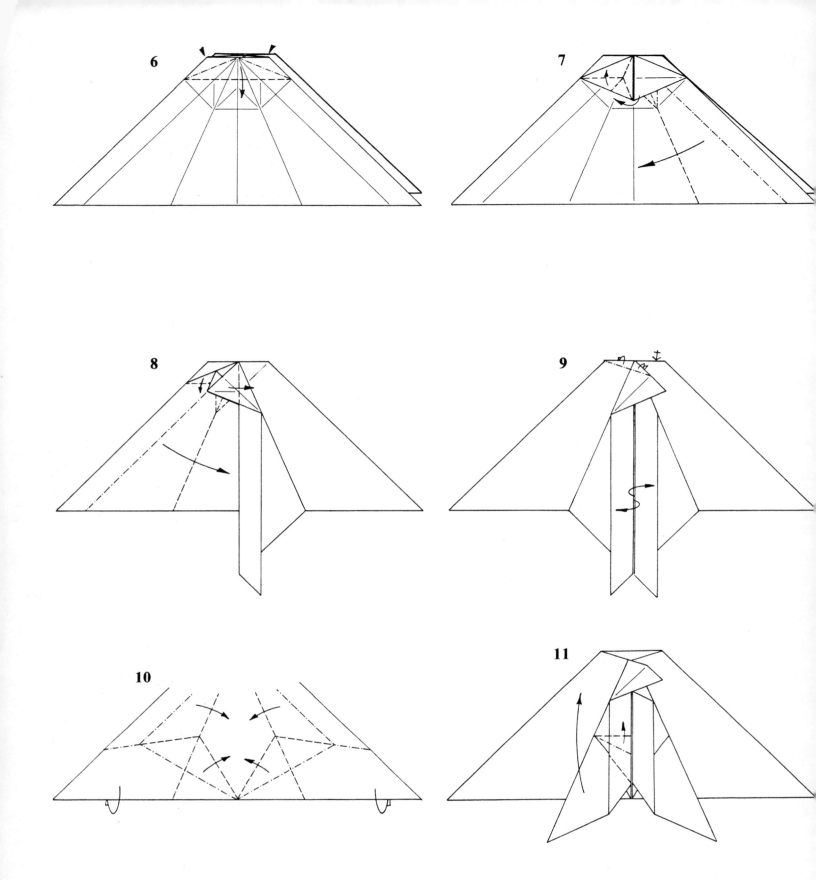

6. Spread-sink two of the top corners on existing creases.

7. Fold the right side of the top layer in on existing creases. The top of the model will pivot clockwise, and it will be necessary to make the folds shown in the left side of the tail.

8. Do the same thing on the left (it's harder the second time).

9. Mountain-fold the trailing edges of the tail. Open out the bottom of the model (but don't unfold the tail; the paper will not lie flat).

10. Form two double rabbit ears. The major creases already exist.

11. Squash-fold the small pocket towards the center.

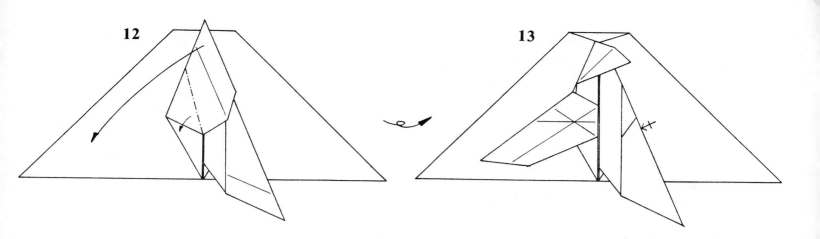

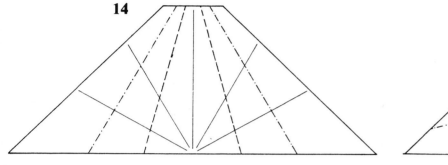

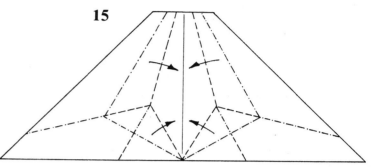

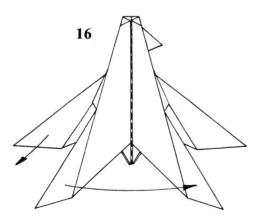

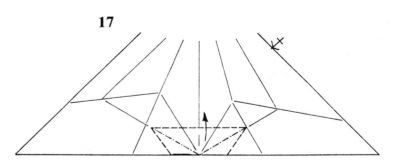

12. Squash and pivot the major part of the wing.

13. Repeat for the right wing. Turn the model over from side to side.

14. Crease the angle trisectors. The corner of the angle is the (imaginary) corner of the truncated triangle.

15. Form two more double rabbit ears. They will not line up exactly with the ones underneath.

16. Take the upper and lower left wings and pull them in opposite directions. Allow the model to start to open up, but don't let the tail come unfolded.

17. Reverse-fold the region shown and refold the model. Repeat behind.

18

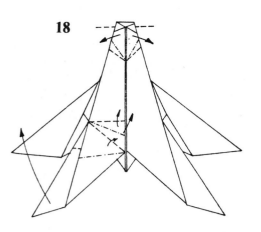

19

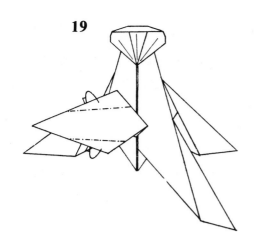

20

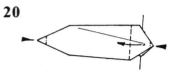

21

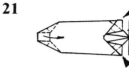

22

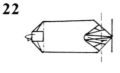

23

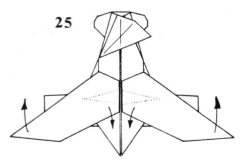

24

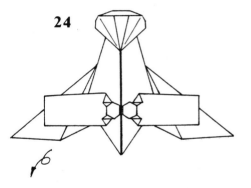

25

26

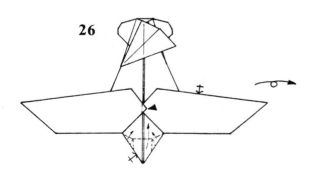

18. Crimp the two small flaps at the top as far apart as is possible. Form two squash folds on the wing.

19. Reverse-fold the sides of the wing underneath.

20. Detail of wing and wheel. Sink the tips of the wing (at the left) and the wheel (at the right). Petal-fold the wheel.

21. Double-reverse-fold the corners of the wing at the wheel. Double-rabbit-ear the tip of the wing.

22. Mountain-fold the tip of the wing behind. Petal-fold the wheel to the center line.

23. Repeat steps 18–22 on the right wing.

24. Turn the model over from side to side.

25. Pivot the wings back so that their leading edges are aligned.

26. Sink the tiny corners of the wings that overlap. Double-rabbit-ear the propeller, both top and bottom. Turn the model over from top to bottom.

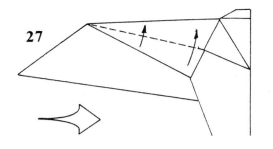

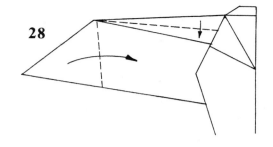

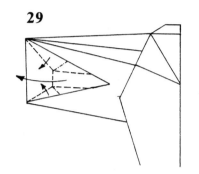

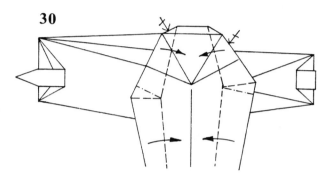

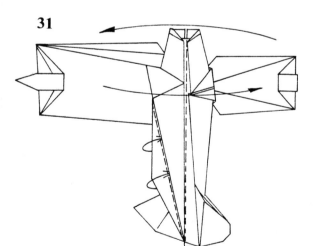

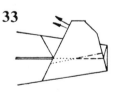

27. Enlarged view of the underside of the upper wing. Valley-fold the layer shown forward.

28. Valley-fold the tip of the wing in. Valley-fold the leading edge of the wing back.

29. Double-rabbit-ear the tip of the wing.

30. This view shows both upper and lower wings. Form the long, narrow rabbit ears to narrow the body.

31. Tuck the loose layer shown into the body. Fold the top wing over in front and the bottom wing over behind.

32. Detail of tail. Sink the tip of the vertical stabilizer.

33. Put a light crimp in the rear of the stabilizer and pull out the layers in front as far as they will go.

34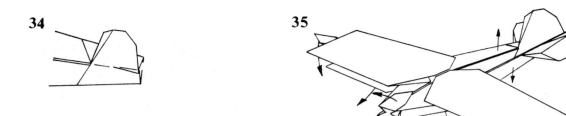

35

36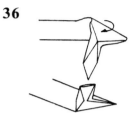

37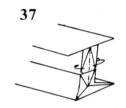

38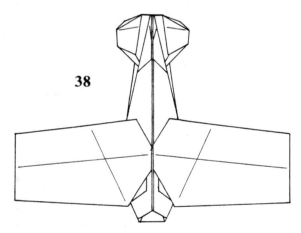

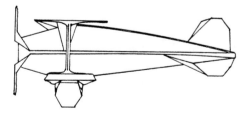

34. Like so.

35. Lift up the propellers away from the body. Open out the fuselage from the front. Bend the wings down away from the underbody (not shown in the drawing). Fold the struts toward each other.

36. Detail of struts. Adjust the length of the upper wing so that the upper and lower struts match up. Insert the upper strut into the corresponding hole in the lower strut.

37. Mountain-fold the strut in half and pinch it.

38. Finished Biplane.

Turtle

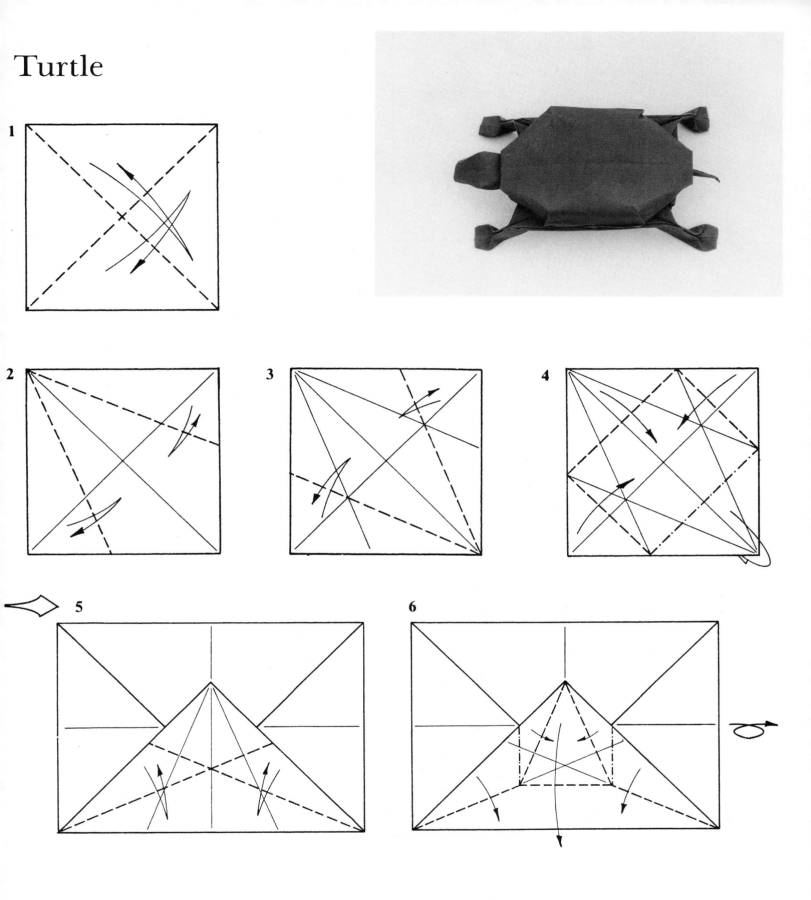

1

2

3

4

5

6

Paper: Use a square, colored side up.

1. Crease both diagonals.

2. Fold two edges in to the center, crease well, and unfold.

3. Fold the other two edges in to lie along the same diagonal.

4. Valley-fold three corners into the middle; mountain-fold the fourth behind. The folds are made from the intersections of the creases of steps 2 and 3 with the edges.

5. Enlarged view. Fold down the left edge of the large triangular flap to lie along its hypotenuse (thus bisecting the angle at the left). Crease and unfold. Repeat for the right edge.

6. Form two connected rabbit ears. Turn the model over.

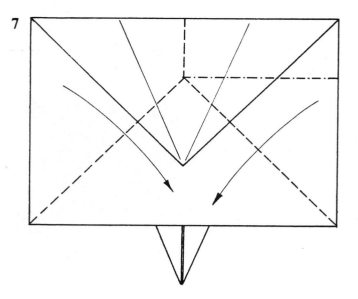

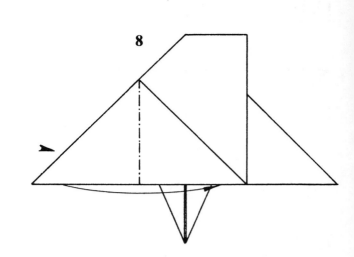

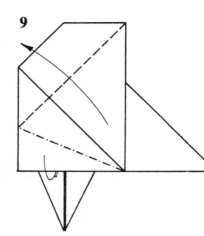

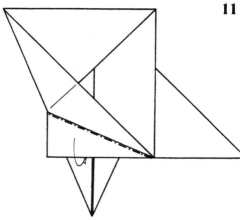

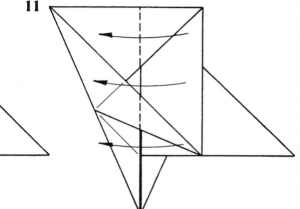

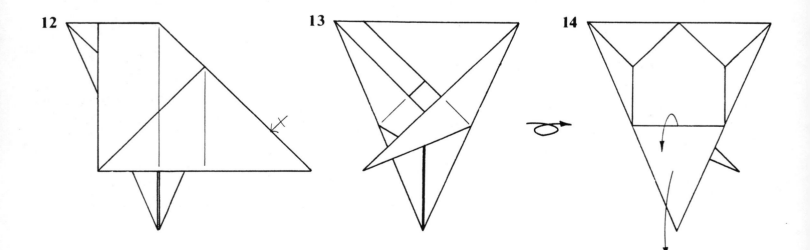

7. Form a large rabbit ear.
8. Reverse-fold the point at the left.
9. Petal-fold.
10. Reverse-fold the edge inside the model.
11. Book-fold the rectangular flap from the right over to the left.

12. Repeat steps 8–10 on the right.
13. Turn the model over.
14. Grasp the bottom point and stretch it downward. The paper will become partially unfolded.

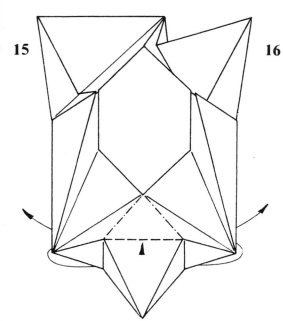

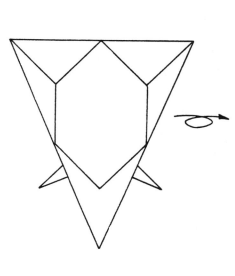

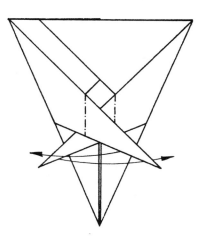

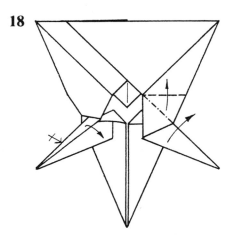

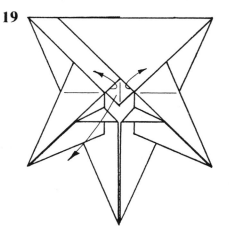

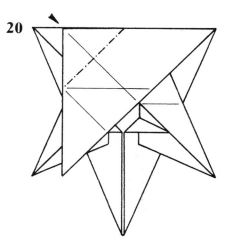

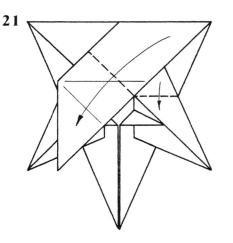

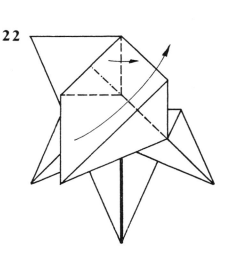

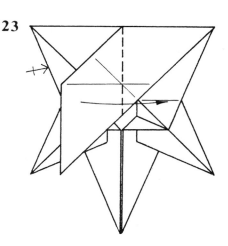

15. Refold the model, but push in the indicated portion and change the indicated creases.

16. Like so. Turn the model back over.

17. Reverse-fold the two points to the outside. A small gusset will form on the inside of the reverse folds.

18. The gusset is visible on the left side. Swivel the flap open as shown on the right. Repeat on the left.

19. Pull the original corner of the square out from the inside of the model.

20. Sink the indicated corner.

21. Valley-fold the upper right corner down to the lower left.

22. Valley-fold the flap back up to the right, but pull out the small triangle along the centerline.

23. Valley-fold the middle flap over to the right and repeat steps 21 and 22 on the left.

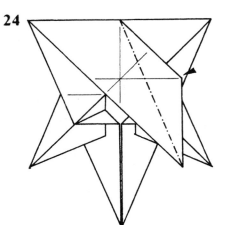

24

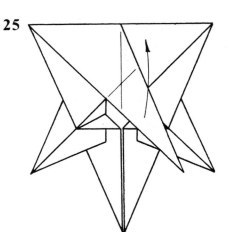

25

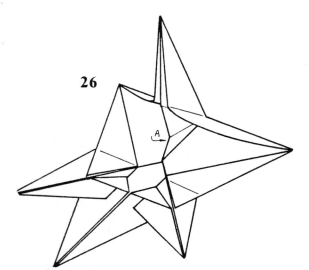

26

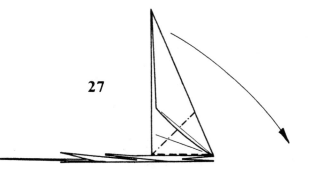

27

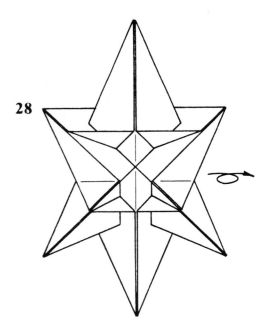

28

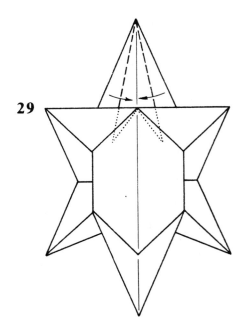

29

24. Closed-sink the blunt triangle.

25. Lift the central flap up away from the model.

26. Perspective view. Since the sink in step 24 was a closed sink, the flap marked A will come untucked easily. The long central point can then be lifted up at right angles to the rest of the model.

27. Side view. Squash-fold the central point symmetrically.

28. Like so. Turn the model over.

29. Valley-fold the edges of the tail in to the center line. The dotted lines show hidden folds.

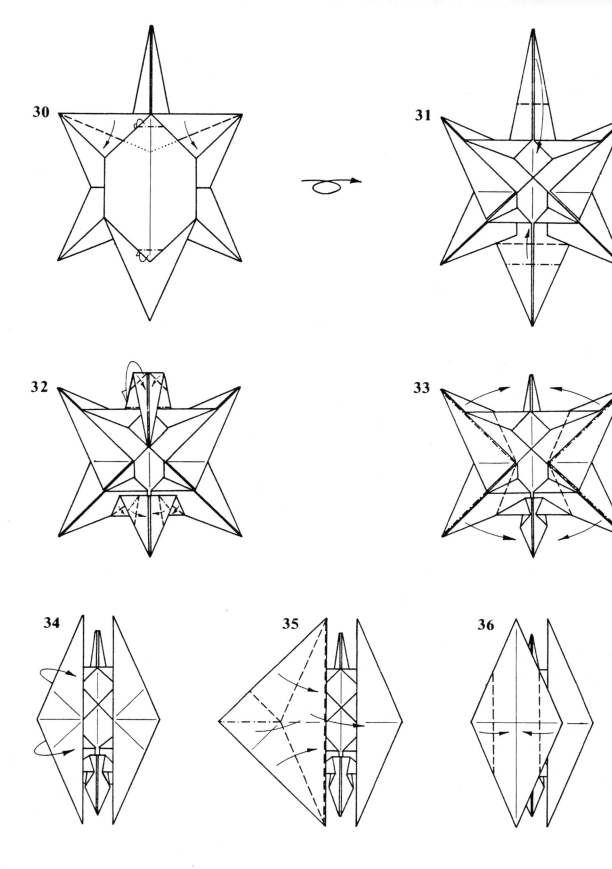

30. Mountain-fold the front and rear corners of the shell (or better yet, closed-sink them). Valley-fold the edges of the rear legs. Turn the model over.

31. Valley-fold the tip of the tail (top point) down to the base of the small square. Crimp the head as indicated.

32. Valley-fold the edges of the tail to make a point. Mountain-fold the tail behind, so that it tucks into the pocket formed by the folds of step 30. Narrow the head with the valley and mountain folds shown.

33. Pivot all four legs in to lie along the vertical. The flap between the front and rear legs will flatten out.

34. Untuck the hidden flaps of paper.

35. Form a rabbit ear, then valley-fold it over to the right.

36. Valley-fold the edges of the diamond-shaped flap into the center.

37

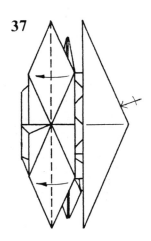

38

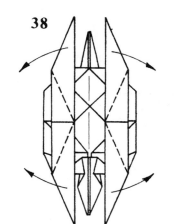

39

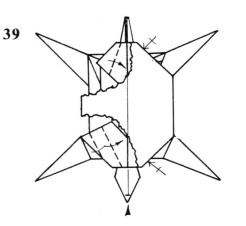

40

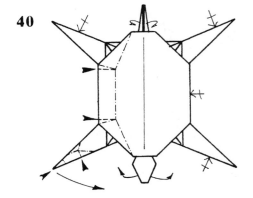

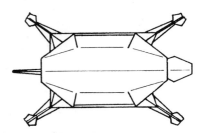

41

37. Fold the leg in half. Repeat steps 34–37 on the right leg.

38. Valley-fold outward all four legs. Turn the model over.

39. Broken-out view. Valley-fold the two flaps near the tail in to the center. They are normally hidden by the shell and you may need to use tweezers. Fold over and over the corresponding flaps near the head. These folds lock the body together.

40. Sink the tip of the left front leg. Sink and pivot the foot at the ankle. Repeat for the other three legs. Mountain-fold the tail in half vertically. Sink slightly the corners of the shell, while pushing the shell up from the inside. The hexagonal hole in the belly facilitates this.

41. Finished Turtle.

Scorpion

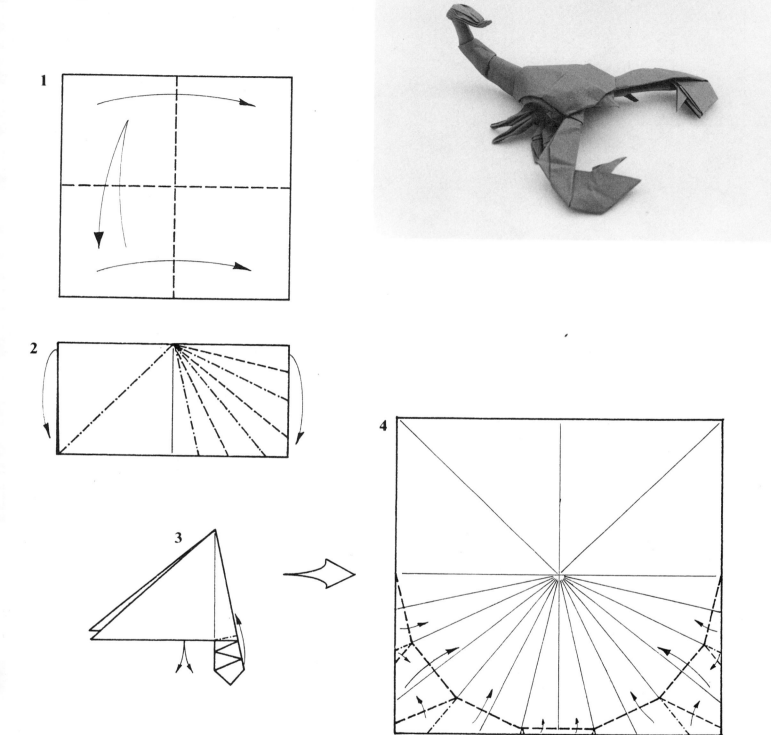

Paper: Use a square of thin paper, white side up.

1. Crease the paper in half vertically, then fold it in half horizontally.

2. Reverse-fold the left corner down along the angle bisector. Pleat the right side, dividing the right angle into seven equal parts.

3. Mountain-fold through all layers. The crease is at right angles to the right edge of the model. Open the paper out completely.

4. Enlarged view. The paper is still white side up. Fold the edges in all the way around. The valley folds lie on the creases made in step 3.

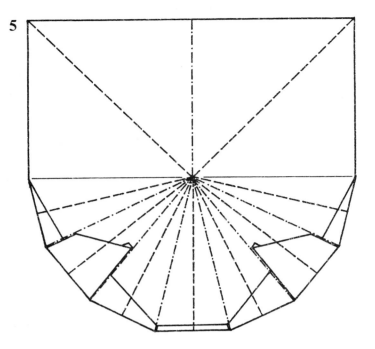

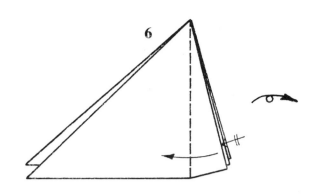

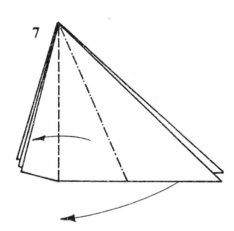

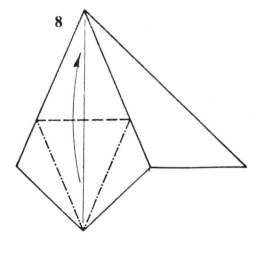

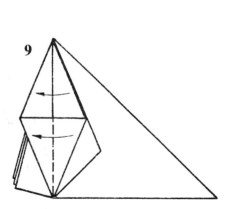

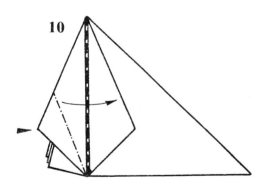

5. Form the creases shown. They all lie on existing creases, but some of them will have to be reversed.

6. Book-fold three layers over to the left. Turn the paper over from side to side.

7. Squash-fold one layer, symmetrically.
8. Petal-fold the flap.
9. Spread-sink the corner.
10. Book-fold one layer to the left.

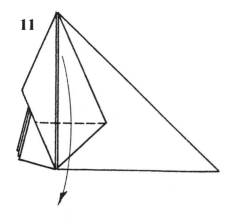

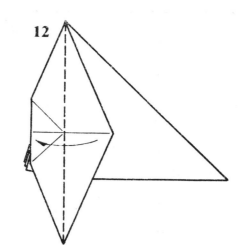

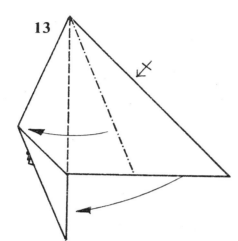

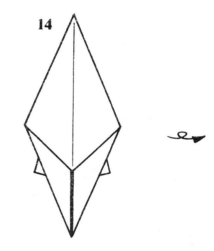

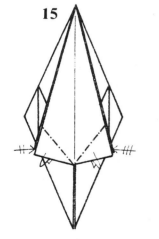

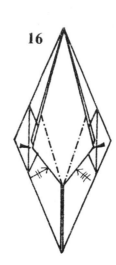

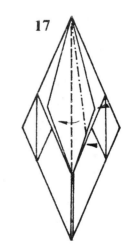

11. Fold one layer of the point from top to bottom, as far as it will go.

12. Book-fold one layer.

13. Repeat steps 7–12 on the right.

14. Like so. Turn the model over from side to side.

15. Reverse-fold seven corners, three on the left and four on the right.

16. Sink seven corners along angle bisectors.

17. Spread-sink one corner on the right.

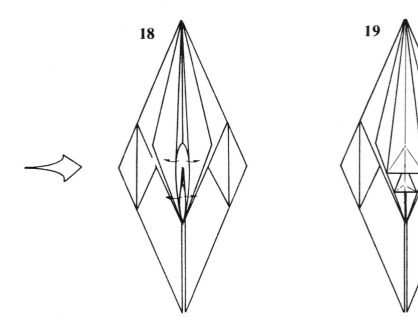

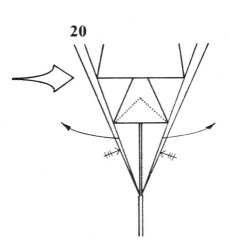

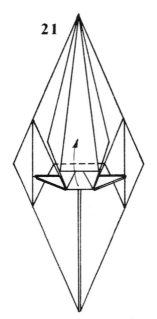

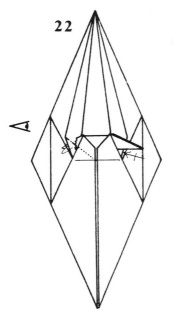

18. Enlarged view. Spread-sink in progress. There is a smaller corner inside that must also be spread-sunk.

19. Spread-sink completed.

20. Enlarged view of legs. Reverse-fold four points on each side as far out as they will go.

21. Valley-fold the entire leg assembly as far up as possible.

22. Mountain-fold the thick bundle of layers under the legs into the interior of the model on both sides.

23. View from 22 of the mountain fold, before . . .

24. . . . and after.

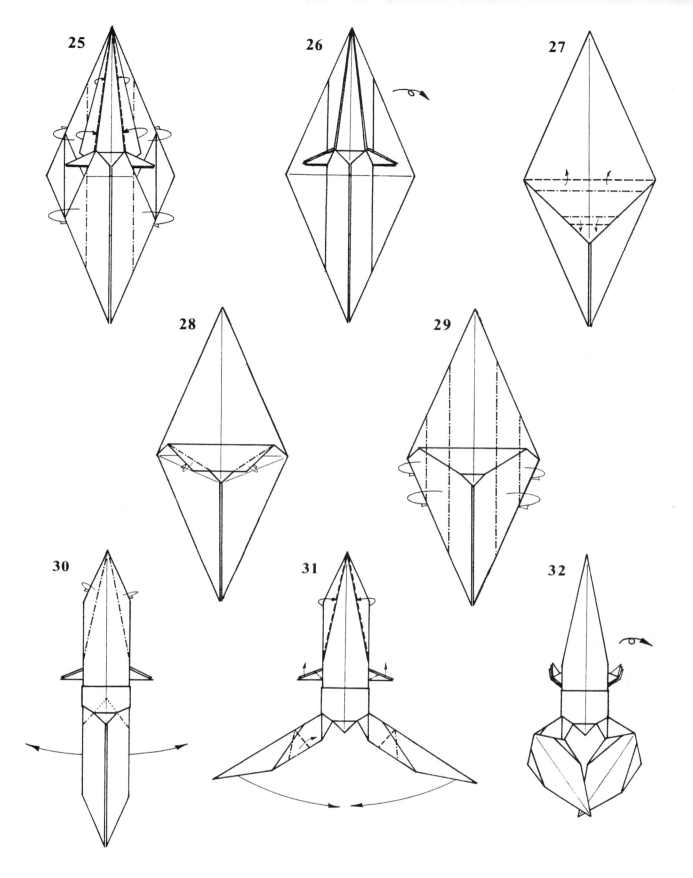

25. Valley-fold all the layers of the tail together as one into the model. Narrow the body with mountain folds.

26. Like so. Turn the model over from side to side.

27. Form two pleats.

28. Note the location of the lower pleat. Mountain-fold the corners of the head.

29. Mountain-fold over and over and tuck the layers inside the model.

30. Mountain-fold the edges of the tail. Reverse-fold the claws.

31. Valley-fold the remaining edges of the tail into the model. Squash-fold the tips of the claws. Reverse-fold all eight legs.

32. Like so. Turn the model over.

33

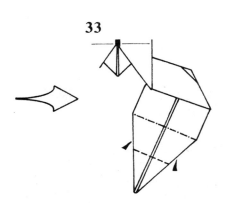

34

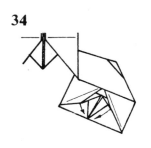

35

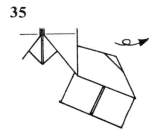

36

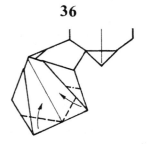

37

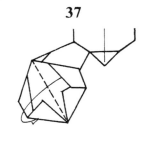

38

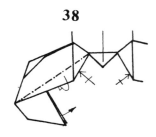

39

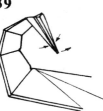

40

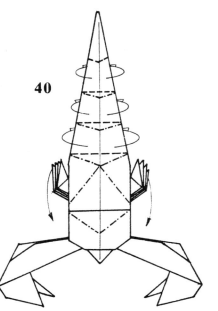

41

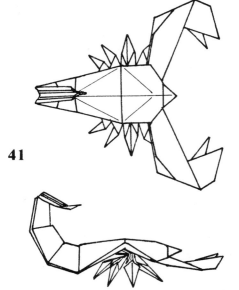

33. Enlarged view of claw. Double-sink the tip of the claw.

34. In progress.

35. Finished double sink. Turn the model over.

36. Valley-fold the left corner and reverse-fold the right corner.

37. Wrap the right half of the claw over the top of the left half.

38. Mountain-fold the leading edge of the claw; repeat underneath. Pull the point out of the interior of the claw. Repeat steps 33–38 on the other claw.

39. Shape the back with mountain folds as shown. Round and crimp the tail.

40. Pinch the tip of the tail to make a stinger.

41. Finished Scorpion.

Tarantula

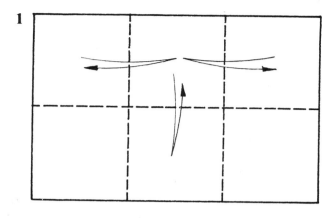

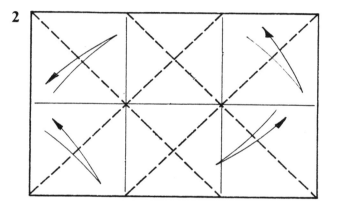

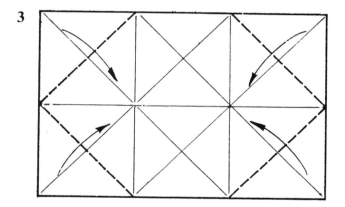

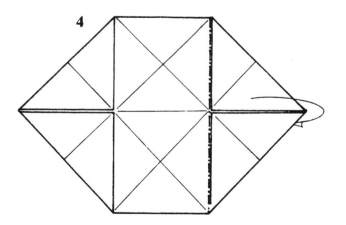

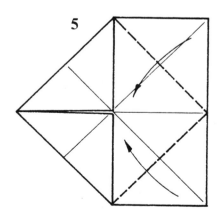

Paper: Use a 1:1.5 rectangle, colored side up.
1. Divide the paper into six equal squares.
2. Add the diagonal creases.

3. Fold the corners in to the center line.
4. Mountain-fold the right side behind.
5. Fold two corners in to the center line.

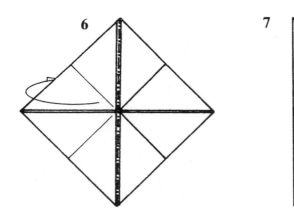

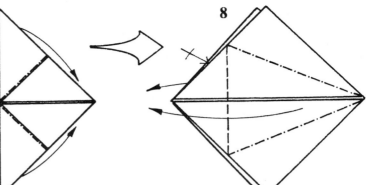

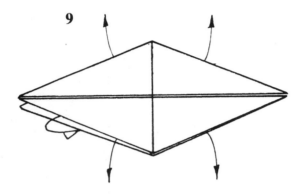

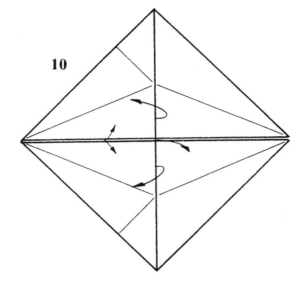

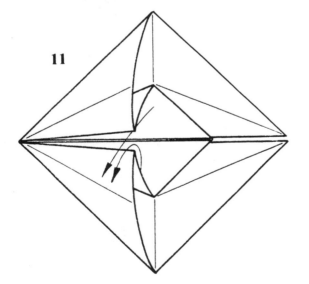

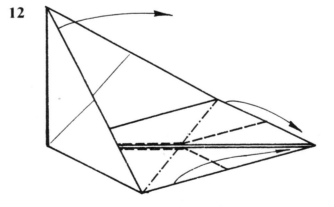

6. Mountain-fold the model in half vertically.

7. Reverse-fold the top and bottom corners.

8. Enlarged view. Petal-fold one flap on both the front and back.

9. Pull out the extra layers of paper. Fold down the point in back.

10. Release more trapped layers.

11. Pull the extra paper up at right angles to the rest of the model.

12. Make a Preliminary Fold with the base of the paper, bringing the pyramidal portion to the right.

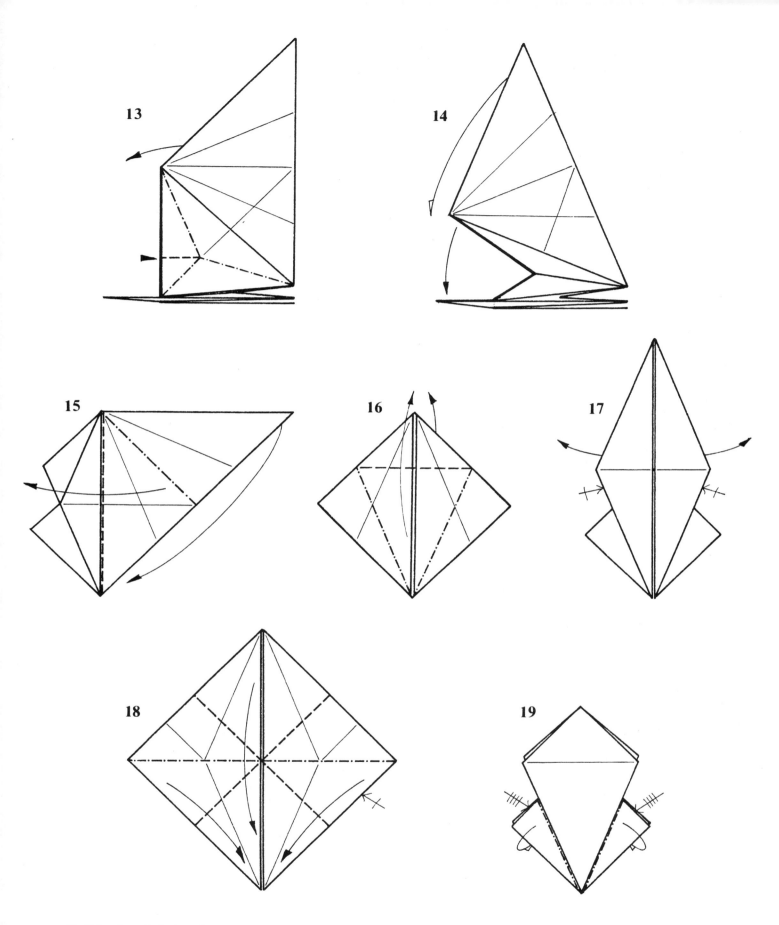

13. Side view. Sink the edge shown.

14. Flatten the model out. Swing the long point at the top over to the left.

15. Squash-fold the long point.

16. Petal-fold in front and lift up the point on the back side.

17. Pull out all the extra layers in both front and back.

18. Make a Preliminary Fold. Repeat behind.

19. Reverse-fold five sets of edges on each side.

20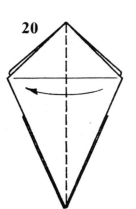

21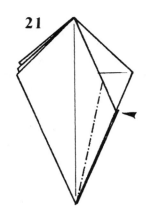

22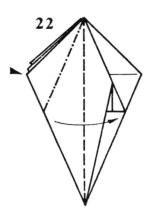

23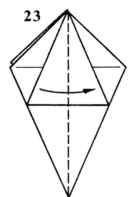

24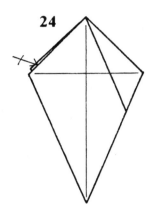

25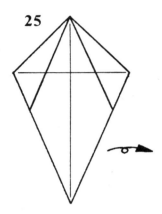

26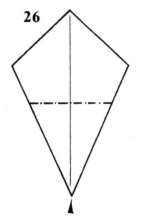

27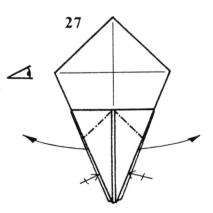

28

20. Book-fold one layer over to the left.
21. Sink the long edge.
22. Spread-sink the left corner.
23. Book-fold one layer from left to right.
24. Repeat steps 20–23 on the left.

25. Like so. Turn the model over from side to side.
26. Sink one point up into the model as far as it will go.
27. Reverse-fold the first and third points on each side.
28. View from 27, showing which points are reversed.

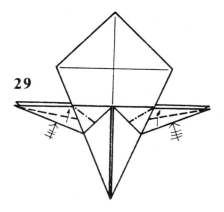 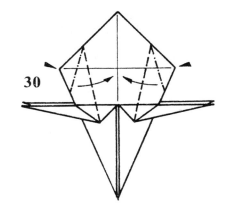 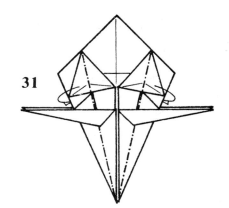

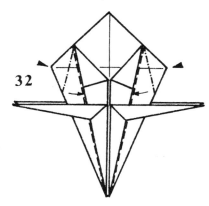 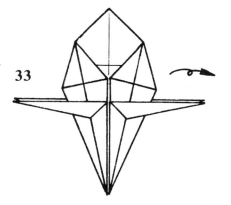 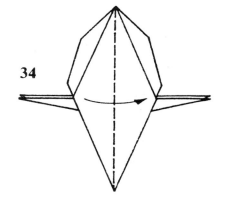

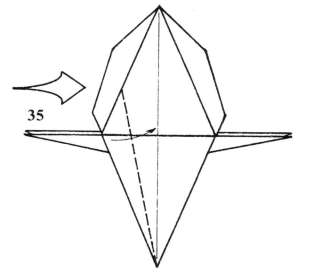 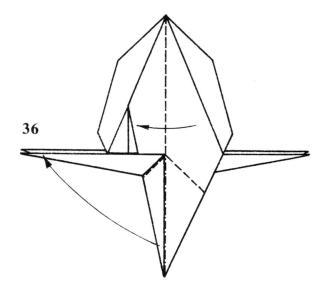

29. Narrow each point with reverse folds. There are a total of eight.

30. Spread-sink two corners.

31. Mountain-fold the long edges behind.

32. Spread-sink the remaining corners.

33. Turn the model over from side to side.

34. Book-fold one layer from left to right.

35. Enlarged view. Valley-fold the long edge into the center.

36. Book-fold one layer, but bring the leg up to match the other two.

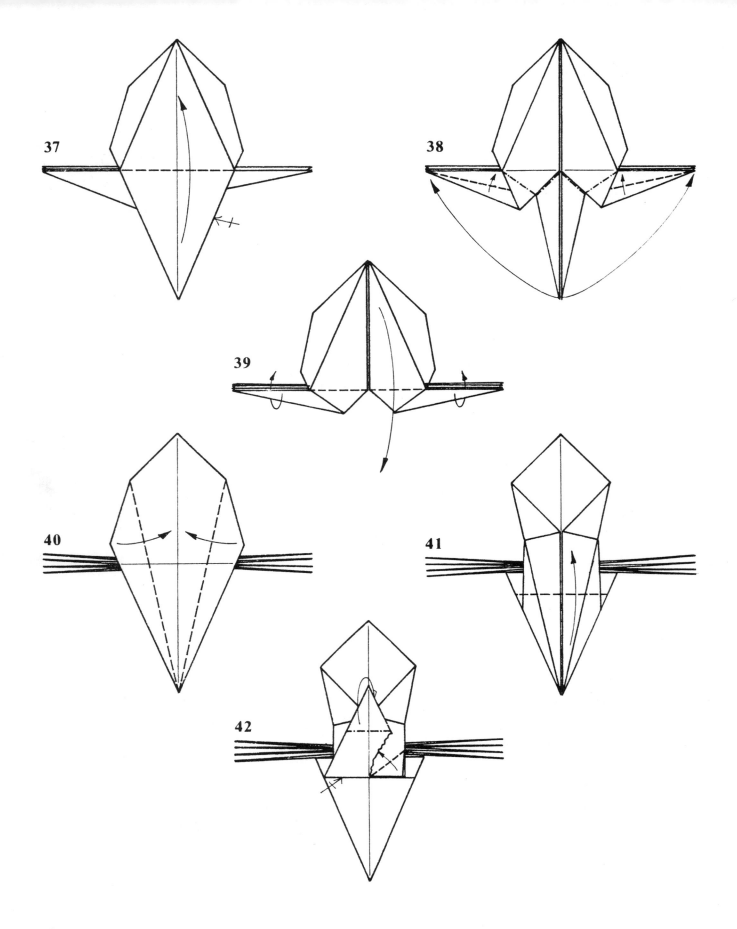

37. Repeat steps 34–36 on the right. Fold the flap at the bottom of the model upwards.

38. Narrow the legs. Reverse-fold the remaining set of legs outward.

39. Fold two points from the top downward and rotate the legs so they are at right angles to the rest of the body.

40. Valley-fold the edges.

41. Valley-fold the thick point.

42. Fold the thick corners in the inside of the model over to lock the result of step 41 into place. Mountain-fold the tip of the head underneath.

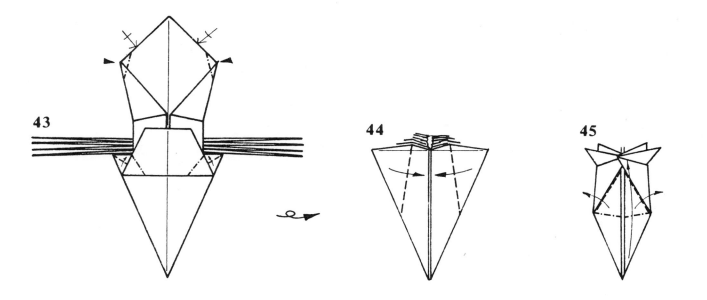

 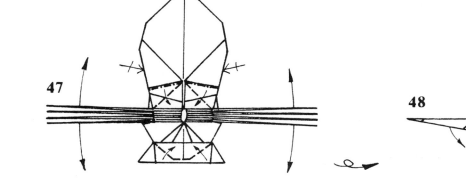 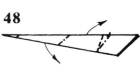

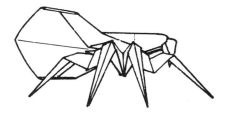 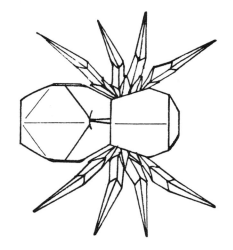

43. Closed-sink the corners of the abdomen. Reverse-fold the corners of the head. Turn the model over.

44. Detail of head. Valley-fold the sides of the head in as far as possible.

45. Open out the edges of the head.

46. Valley-fold.

47. Crimp the point where the head and abdomen join; the abdomen will puff out. Spread the legs. Rabbit-ear the head to give fangs.

48. Crimp and reverse-fold the legs.

49. Finished Tarantula.

Cicada

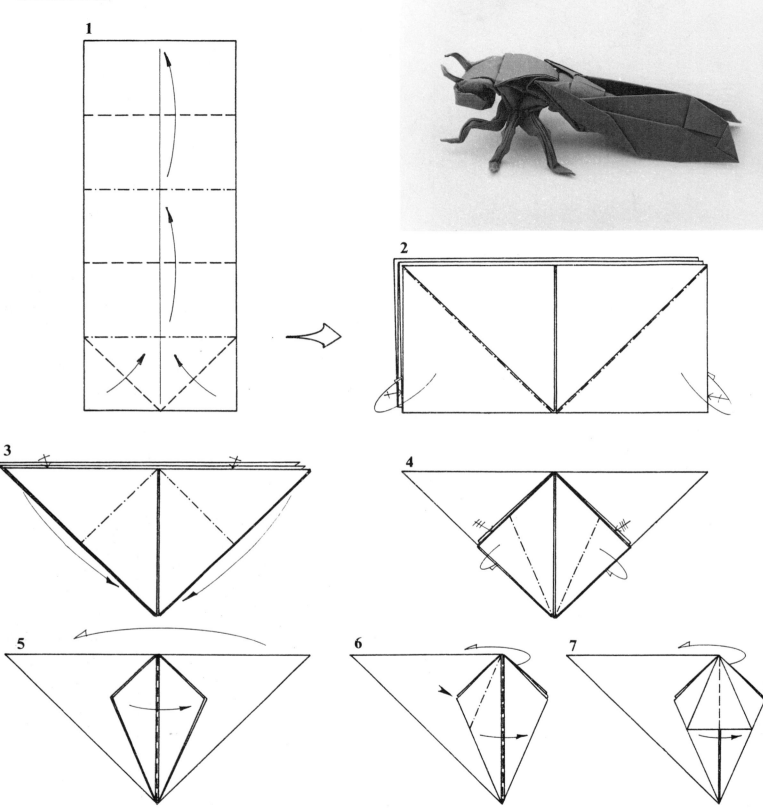

Paper: Use a 1:2.5 rectangle of thin paper.

1. Pleat the paper into fifths the long way. Fold the bottom corners to the center.

2. Enlarged view. Reverse-fold the corners in on both sides. Repeat behind.

3. Reverse-fold four corners down.

4. Reverse-fold the edges in eight places.

5. Book-fold one layer from left to right in front, and one from right to left in back (to keep the same number of thicknesses on both sides).

6. Spread-sink one corner in front. Book-fold one layer behind to compensate for the extra thickness.

7. Book-fold one layer, front and behind.

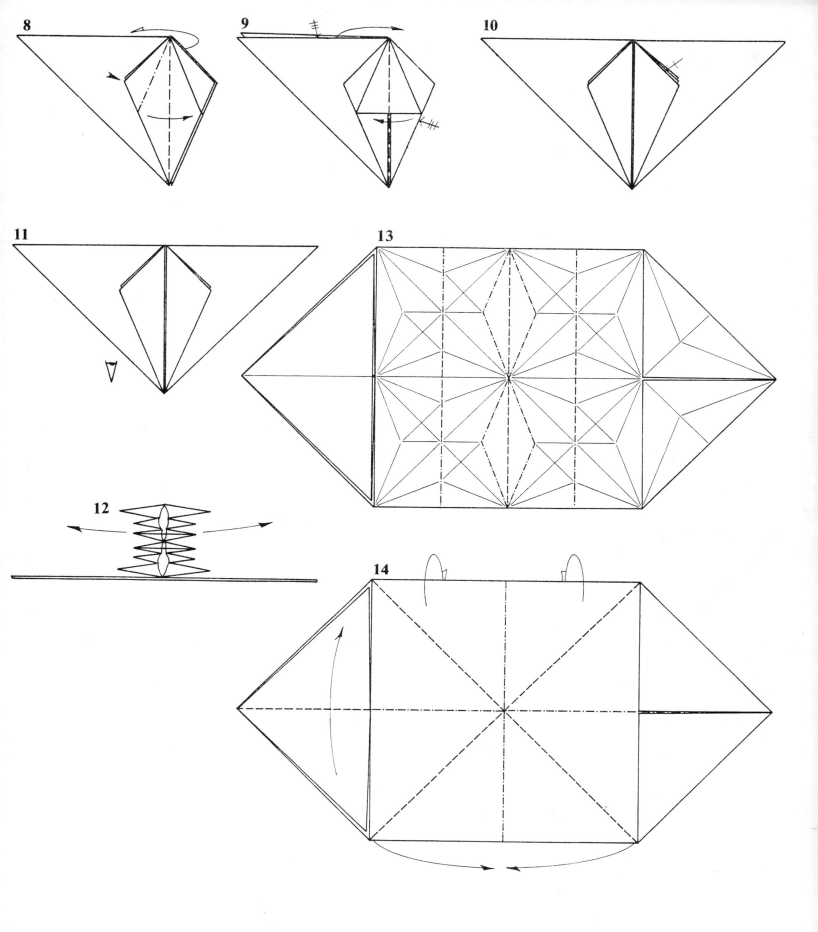

8. Spread-sink another corner. Book-fold one layer behind.

9. Book-fold four layers to the left in front, and four to the right behind.

10. Repeat steps 5–9 on the right.

11. The result looks like this in front.

12. View from 11. Unfold the paper, leaving the corners folded at one end and the Waterbomb Base at the other.

13. Add (or reverse) the creases shown, as necessary.

14. Fold a Preliminary Fold with the central region.

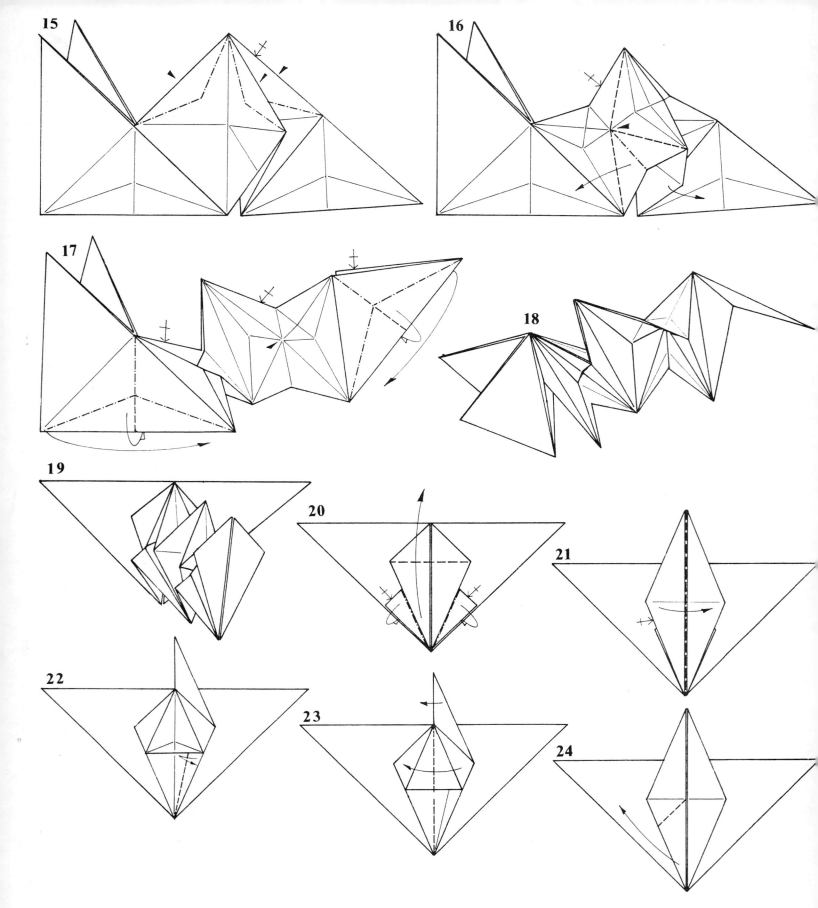

15. Sink the edges shown on existing creases (there are four of them).

16. Push in where indicated and spread apart the edges shown, on both the front and the back.

17. Continue collapsing the model. Squash-fold the two ends.

18. Bring the left and right parts together, flattening things out as you go.

19. Almost there.

20. Flattened. Reverse-fold the small edges at the bottom and lift up one layer in front.

21. Fold two layers over to the right.

22. Crease the edge partially covered by the triangular "hood."

23. Fold two layers back to the left.

24. Lift up the bottom point at 45 degrees.

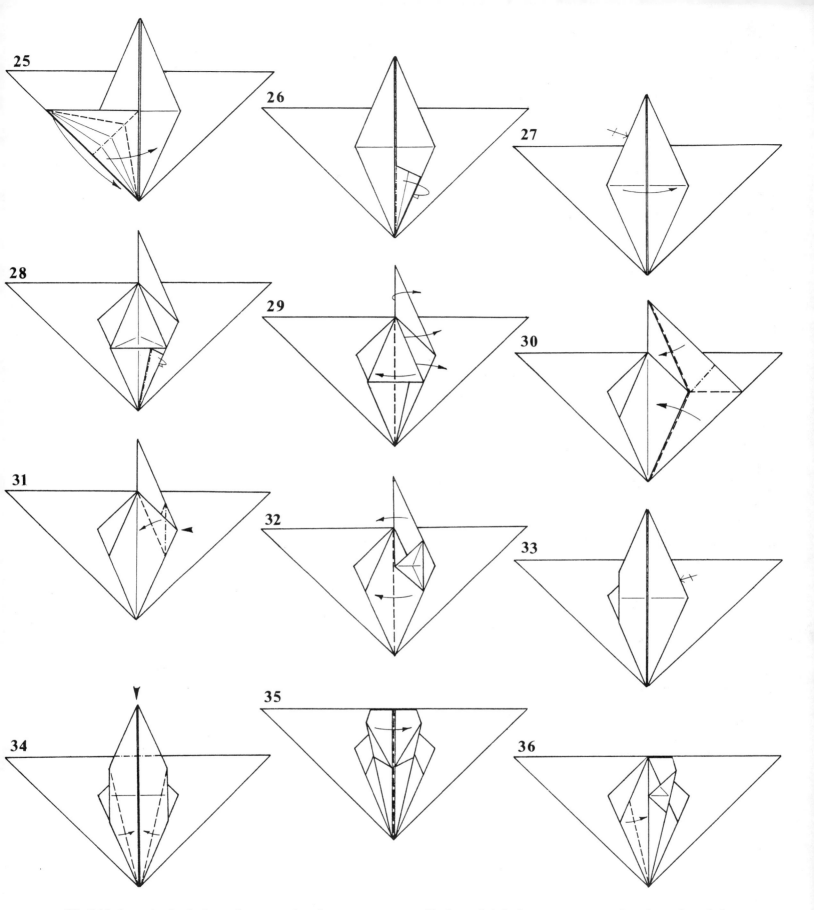

25. Fold the point back down, incorporating the reverse fold made on the creases formed in step 22.

26. Reverse-fold the edge back to the left.

27. Fold two layers over to the right.

28. Reverse-fold the edge in to the center.

29. Fold one layer over to the left, and pull out the extra layers of paper.

30. Form a rabbit ear over the layers shown.

31. Spread-sink the corner, narrowing the point of the rabbit ear.

32. Fold one layer over to the left.

33. Repeat steps 21–32 on the right side.

34. Valley-fold the edges in to the center. Sink the tip down into the interior.

35. Fold one layer over to the right.

36. Valley-fold an edge in to the center line.

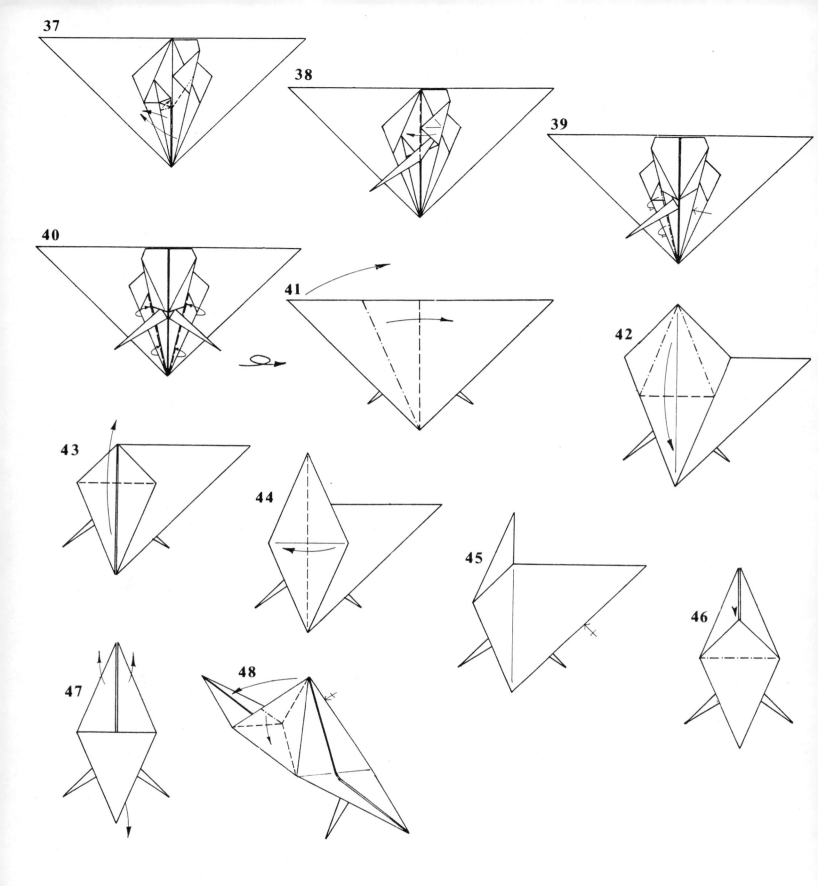

37. Rabbit-ear the long, skinny point.

38. Fold one layer back over to the left.

39. Mountain-fold one layer underneath. Repeat steps 35–39 on the right.

40. Valley-fold the edges inside. Turn the model over from side to side.

41. Squash-fold the large triangle.

42. Petal-fold the tip.

43. Lift the petal fold back up.

44. Fold one layer over to the left.

45. Repeat steps 41–44 on the right.

46. Sink the triangular point down into the model.

47. Grasp the two points at the top and the second layer down at the bottom, and stretch the model. The first layer at the bottom forms a four-sided pyramid.

48. Sink the sides of the pyramid and flatten things out.

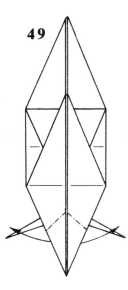
49

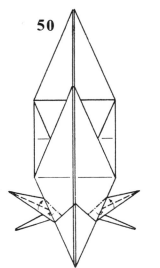
50 **51**

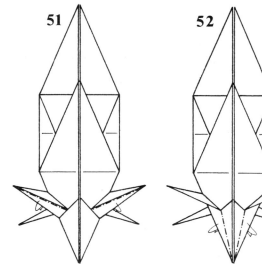
52 **53**

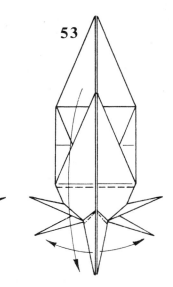

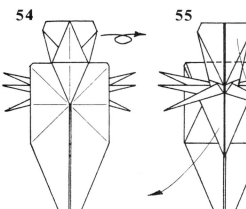
54 **55**

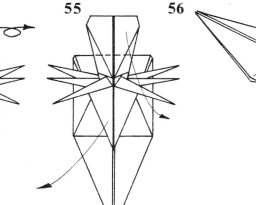
56

57

58

59

60

61

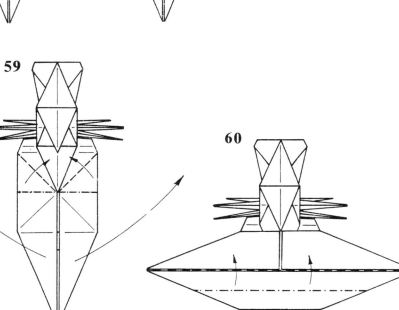

49. Reverse-fold the bottom pair of points out to run slightly above horizontal.

50. Narrow the legs with reverse folds.

51. Reverse-fold the back sides of the legs.

52. Narrow the downward-pointing legs with mountain folds.

53. Reverse-fold the middle legs outward. Valley-fold the long part at the top down as far as it will go.

54. Turn the model over from side to side.

55. Fold the small flap at the top down as far as it will go, crease well, and then take it and the long part in back and

stretch the model as in step 47. This one is harder, however, and must be helped along. Tweezers will also help.

56. Sharpen up the edges of the pyramid formed in the back of the insect. The legs are at right angles to the rest of the fold.

57. Side view. Sink the left side of the pyramid, and pinch the base of the legs.

58. Like so.

59. Pivot the long, skinny points outwards.

60. Pleat the lower edge of the wings.

61. Valley-fold the left wing down.

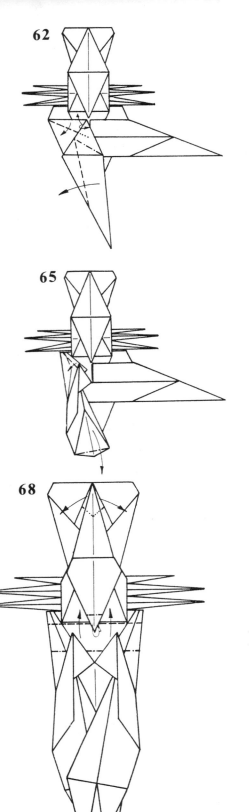
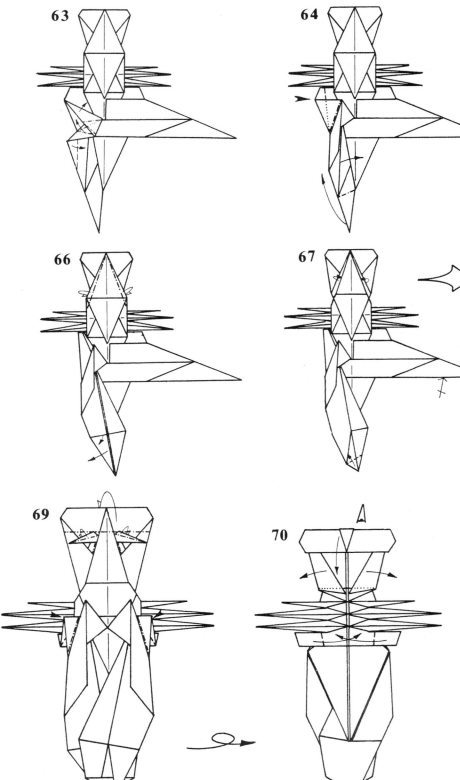

62. Fold over the right side of the wing (both layers). The bottom end of the valley fold terminates directly over the tip of the abdomen. At the same time, squash-fold the upper end of the wing.

63. Fold the left edge of the wing over to lie along the edge of the top layer that cuts across it. At the same time, lift up the forward part of the wing and swivel-fold.

64. Sink the corner of the junction between wing and body. Open the wing up and fold its tip upwards.

65. Fold the tip of the wing back down as far as it will go. Reverse-fold the tiny edge at the upper end of the wing.

66. Mountain-fold the edges along the head. Pull out the trapped paper at the end of the wing.

67. Valley-fold the edges of the head in. Tuck the corner of the wing into the pocket shown. Repeat steps 61–67 on the right wing.

68. Enlarged view. Valley-fold the antennae outward. Mountain-fold underneath the tip of the thorax. Crimp the abdomen and wings up over the thorax.

69. Mountain-fold the tip of the head. Narrow the antennae with mountain folds. Reverse-fold the corners of the wings. Turn the model over from side to side.

70. Fold the head down and pull the layers out from the center line. Fold the sides of the abdomen in as far as possible.

71

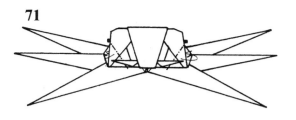

72

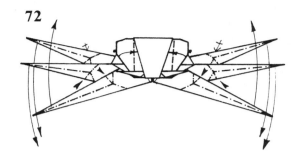

73

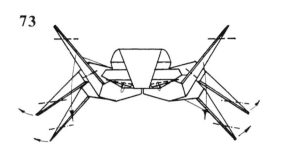

74

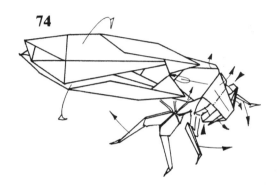

75

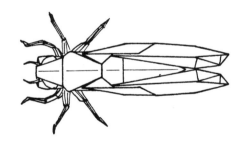

71. View from 70. Reverse-fold the corners of the head.

72. Tuck the layers shown underneath the flap running down the middle of the head. Double-rabbit-ear all the legs.

73. Reverse-fold the legs. Pinch the antennae in half.

74. Round the body and wings. Fan out the legs. Move the antennae forward and squash the eyes. Round the top of the head with the mountain folds shown. Pull out the tip of the thorax, fluff it up, and tuck the tip into the pocket shown.

75. Finished Cicada.

The fourth dimension—time—is incorporated into a fold by giving it motion. In these folds, when two parts of the model are pulled, a different part moves in a way typical of the subject; a bird flaps, a ship rows, or a violinist fiddles. The requirements of the action mechanism generally make the model three-dimensional, so you have all of the complexities of the last chapter. In addition, you must devote special attention to the action mechanism itself. The folds must be precise or the model will at best simply not work and at worst may rip apart when you try to make it work. Your choice of paper will also affect matters. Thick papers don't make very good action models as a rule, and weak papers are likely to tear under the strain of the motion. While the first few models have no particular difficulty, the later ones are quite hard. The instrumentalists, in particular, will tax your skill; the results, however, should be worth your effort.

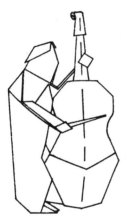

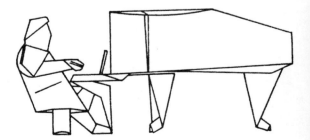

Seagull

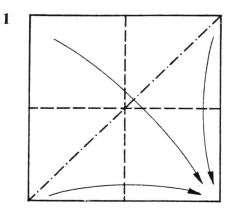

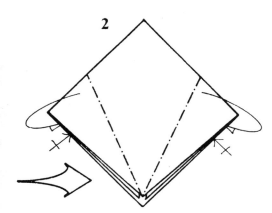

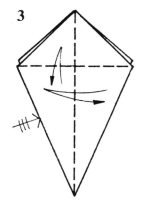

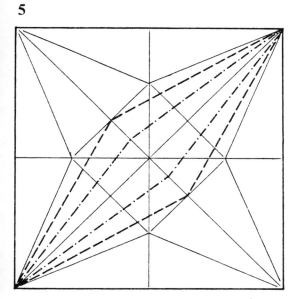

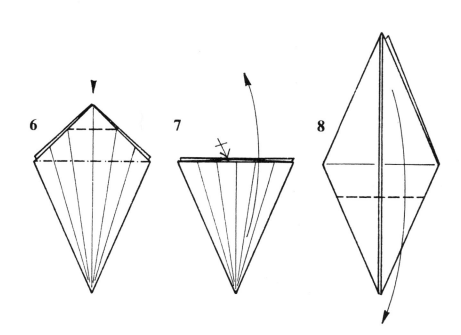

Paper: Use a square, white side up.

1. Make a Preliminary Fold.

2. Enlarged view. Reverse-fold the corners to make a Bird Base.

3. Crease where shown. Repeat on the back and sides.

4. Open the paper out flat.

5. Add the creases shown. First make the valley folds that connect the corners to the points on the diagonals. Then make the mountain folds, which bisect the angles formed by the valley folds and the other diagonal crease. Refold the Bird Base.

6. Double-sink. Note the location of the upper sink fold.

7. Lift up one layer in front and in back.

8. Fold down one flap as far as possible.

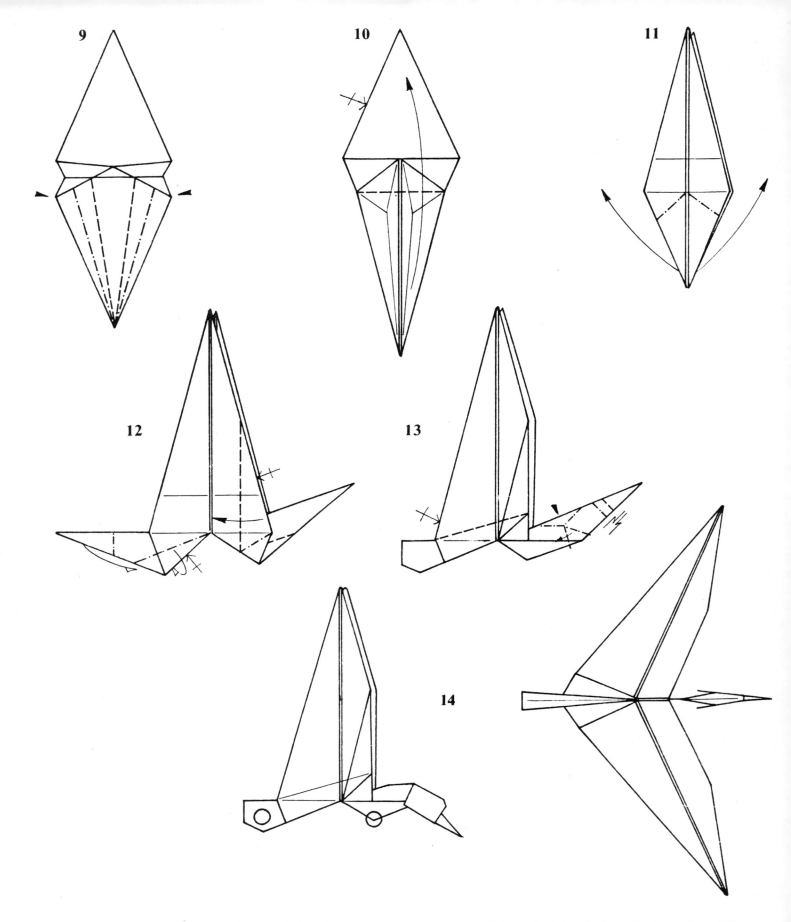

9. Spread-sink the corners. The spread sinks form on existing creases and run all the way to the tips of the wings.

10. Lift the flap back up and repeat steps 8–10 on the other side.

11. Reverse-fold both points.

12. Reverse-fold the tip of the tail. Mountain-fold the bottom edges of the tail. Swivel-fold the leading edge of the wing. Repeat behind.

13. Crease the wing. Crimp the head in two places to make the head and beak.

14. Finished Seagull. Hold at the circles and pull to make the Seagull flap.

Monkey

1

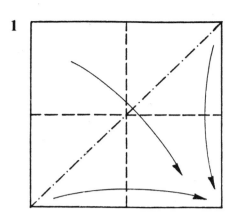

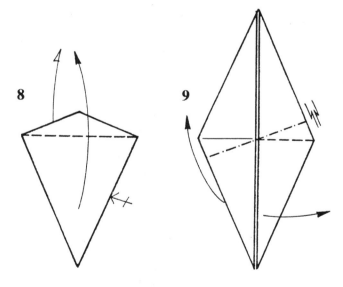

2

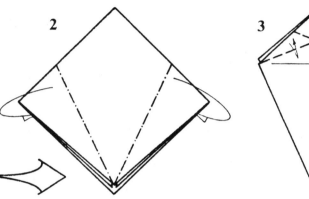

3

4

5

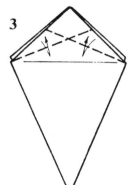

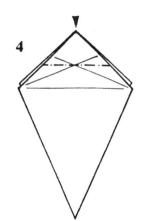

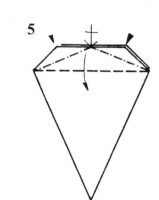

6

7

8

9

Paper: Use a square, white side up.
1. Make a Preliminary Fold.
2. Enlarged view. Reverse-fold the corners to make a Bird Base.
3. Crease the angle bisectors.
4. Sink the tip.
5. Spread-sink the corners. Repeat behind.

6. Valley-fold the corner back up. Repeat behind.
7. Sink the tiny point in the middle of the model back upwards.
8. Valley-fold one layer both in front and behind.
9. Reverse-fold the left point. Crimp the right point. Rotate the model 90 degrees clockwise.

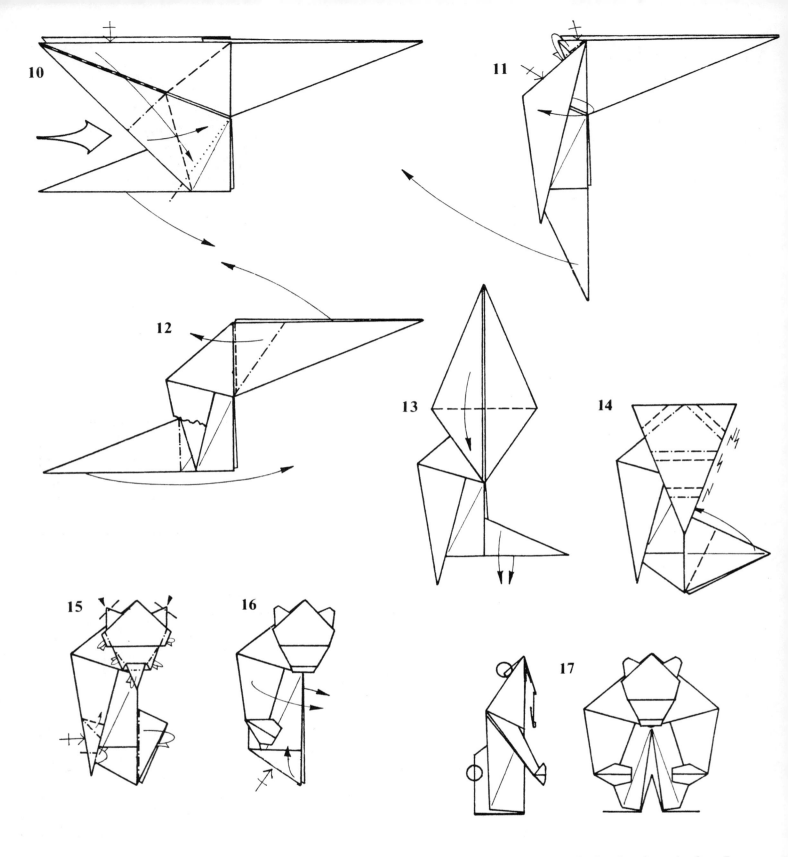

10. Enlarged view. Rabbit-ear the arms (the two points to the right). Repeat behind. Reverse-fold the point at the bottom left.

11. Mountain-fold the tiny corners at the top inside the model. Repeat behind. Undo the reverse fold at the bottom. Wrap the inside of the arm around to the outside. Repeat behind.

12. Squash-fold the point at the top. Reverse-fold the point at the bottom to the right.

13. Valley-fold the tip of the head down. Pull down the outer layers of paper in the feet.

14. Crimp the ears. Pleat the head to form the face. Reverse-fold the feet.

15. Crimp the paws and reverse-fold their tips. Shape the head with mountain folds. Blunt the ears. Reverse-fold the front of the feet.

16. Fold the feet out flat and open up the front of the body.

17. Finished Monkey. Hold at the circles and pull them away from each other. The Monkey will clap his hands.

Viking Ship

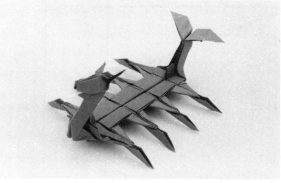

1

2

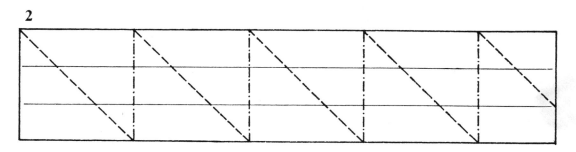

3

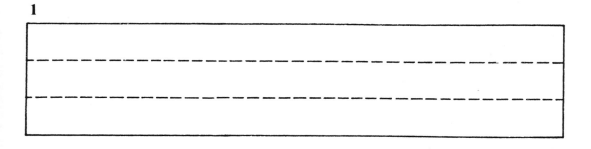

4

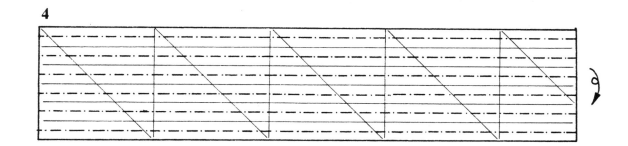

Paper: Use a 1:4.667 rectangle, colored side up.
1. Crease the paper into thirds along the long dimension.
2. Fold 4⅔ squares with diagonals and verticals.

3. Add horizontal creases.
4. Add more horizontal creases.

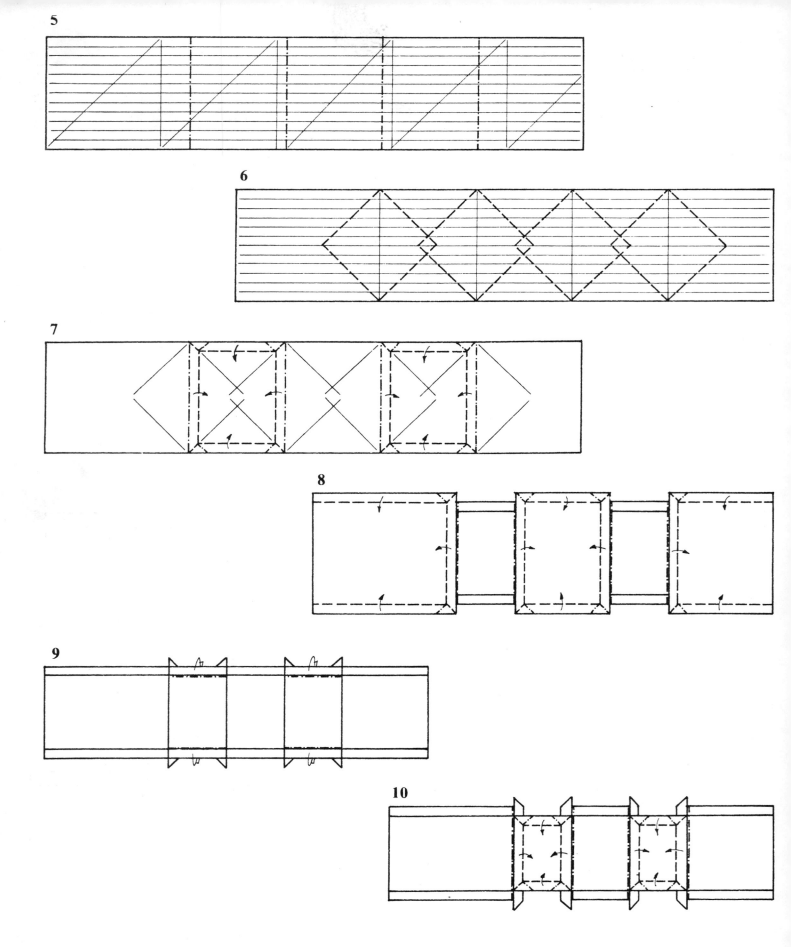

5. Make the vertical folds through the intersections shown. From now on, these will be the vertical reference lines.

6. Add diagonals around the creases made in step 5.

7. Fold the edges shown on existing creases.

8. Do the same thing in the in-between regions of paper.

9. Reverse-fold the edges.

10. Again.

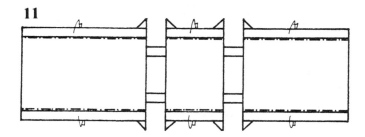

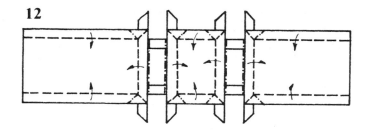

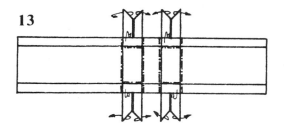

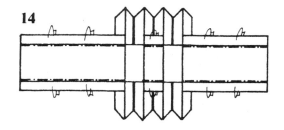

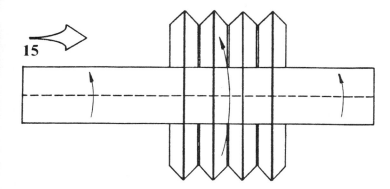

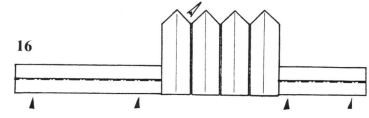

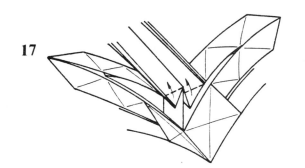

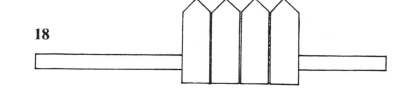

11. Again.
12. Again.
13. Again. Open out the vertical points.
14. And again.
15. Enlarged view. Fold the model in half.

16. Sink the long edge upwards.
17. View from 16, showing details of the termination of the sink. Reverse-fold the indicated corners upward. Do this for both sinks.
18. Like so.

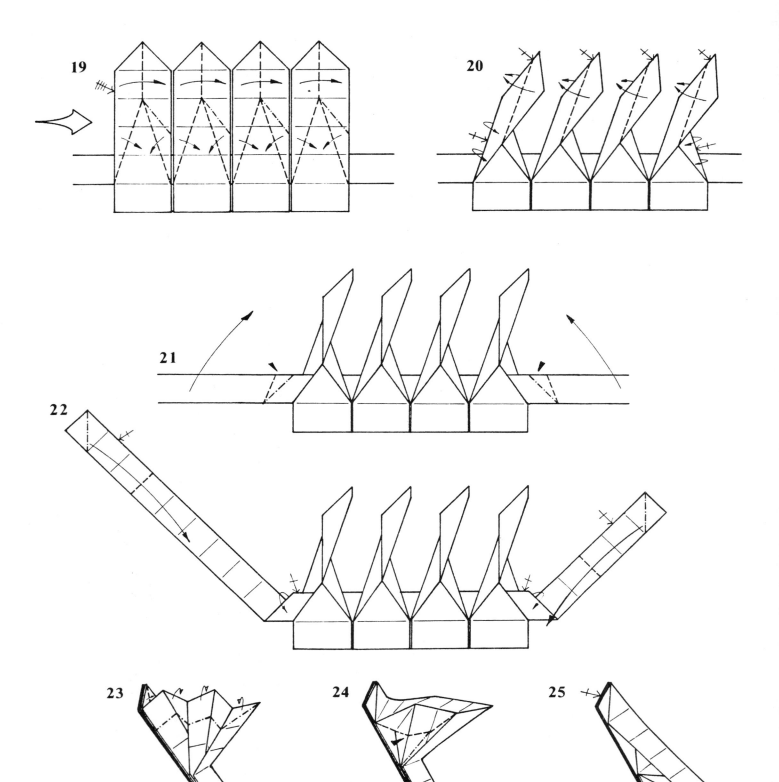

19. Enlarged view. Rabbit-ear the oars. Repeat behind.

20. Outside-reverse-fold the tips of the oars. On the two end oars, wrap all layers from the inside to the outside. Repeat behind.

21. Crimp upwards the long sections of the paper.

22. Elias-stretch the left side of the model. This procedure is illustrated in steps 23–25. Pull all of the layers of paper out of the crimp where the neck joins the oars. Repeat both behind and on the rear (the right) of the boat.

23. Spread the fan apart and fold over one square's width of paper.

24. Sink the indicated edge and flatten out the paper.

25. Elias stretch completed. Repeat on the other side, and at the rear of the boat.

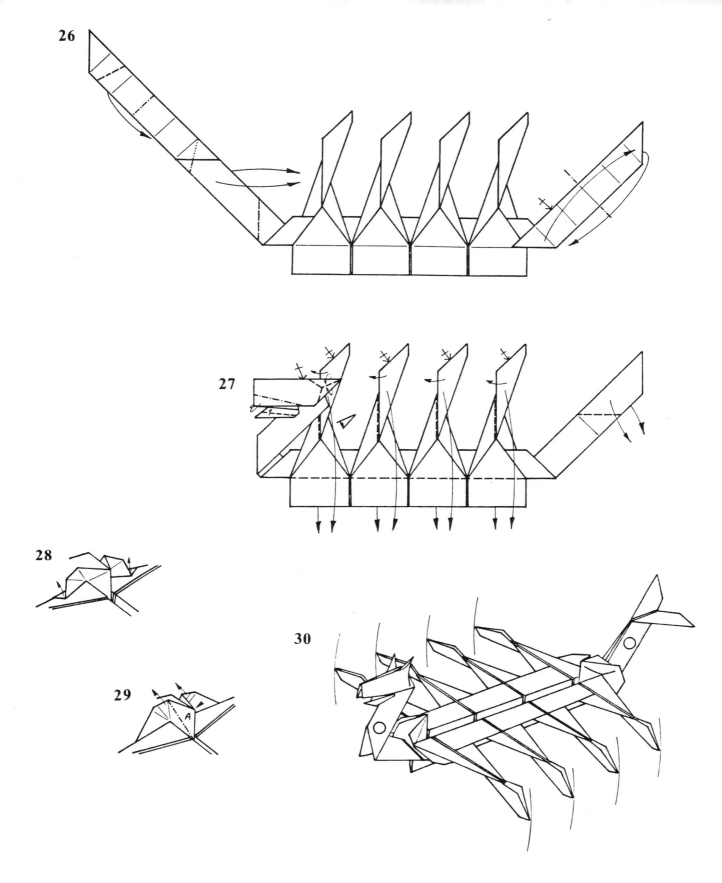

26. Reverse-fold the head and neck. At the rear, reverse-fold the rightmost point down into the inside of the model and swing the two "stretched" points back up.

27. Mountain-fold the edges of the nose. Reverse-fold the lower jaw. Pinch the ears. Swing the oars out at right angles to the boat, and valley-fold the entire oar assembly down as one. Fold it back and forth several times to weaken the paper, so the oar assembly can easily swing up and down. Valley-fold the sides of the tail out flat.

28. View from 27. Pull forward the pockets shown.

29. Gently push down the little pyramid so that the mountain folds form and the region marked A is flat. This step is crucial to getting a rowing action. If there are any folds in region A, the ship will not row very well, if at all.

30. Finished Viking Ship. Hold the neck and tail and pull. The oars will bob up and down.

Violinist

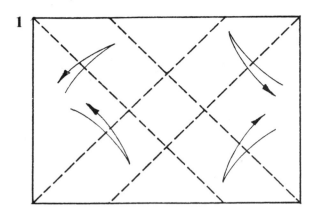

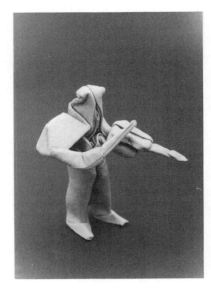

1

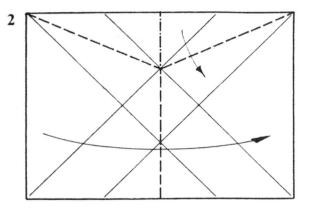

2

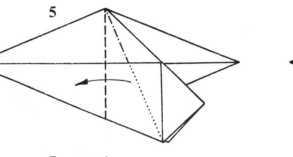

3

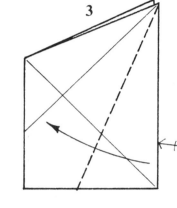

4

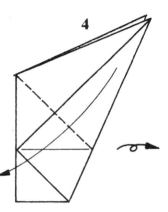

5

6

7

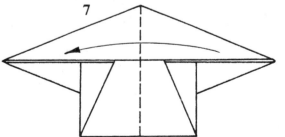

8

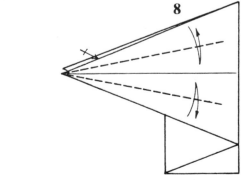

Paper: Use a 1:1.414 rectangle, colored side up.

1. Crease the angle bisectors at all four corners.

2. Fold the left side over and reverse-fold the middle of the top edge.

3. Fold the right edge up to the diagonal. Repeat behind.

4. Fold the long point down to the left on an existing crease. Turn the paper over.

5. Squash-fold the flap shown.

6. Wrap one layer around in front.

7. Fold the model in half.

8. Crease the angle bisectors. Repeat behind.

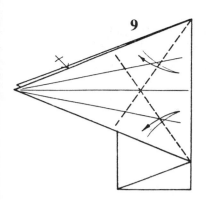

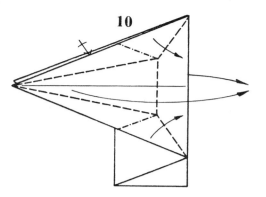

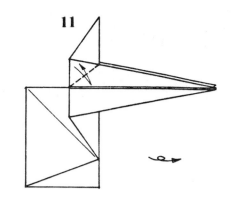

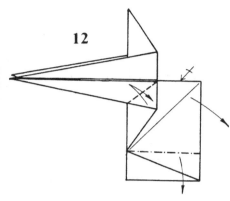

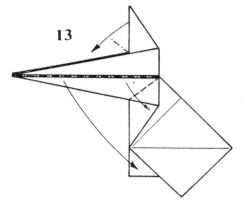

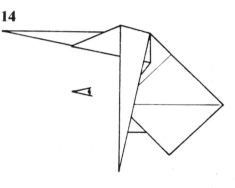

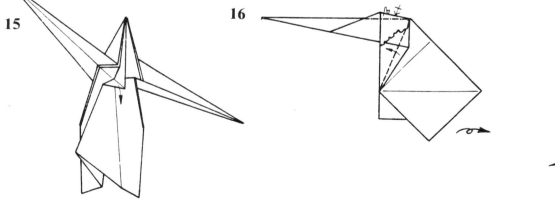

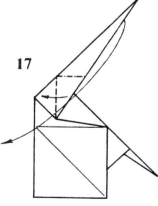

9. Crease two more angle bisectors. Repeat behind.

10. Double-rabbit-ear the point on existing creases. Repeat behind.

11. Crease where shown. Turn the model over.

12. Crease where shown. Pull the layers at the right as far out as they will come.

13. Crimp the model forward. Because of the odd number of layers, you will have to divide them unevenly.

14. Like so.

15. View from 14. Separate the middle layer from the others.

16. Mountain-fold the top edges inside. Valley-fold upward the blunt triangle under the arm. Turn the model over.

17. Squash-fold the arm.

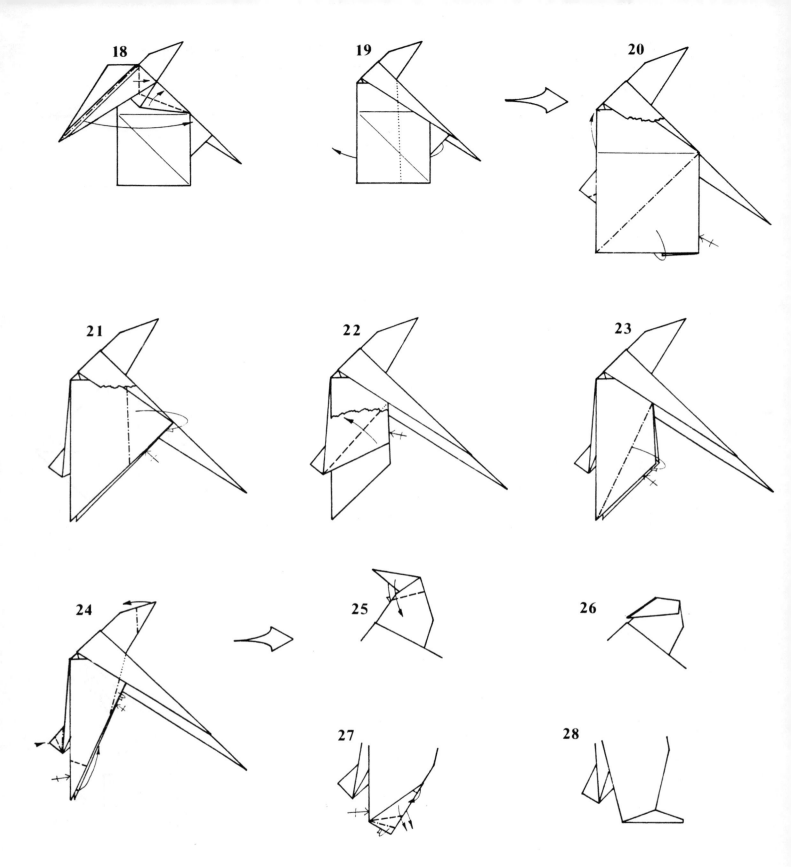

18. Fold up the blunt triangle under the arm. Pinch the arm and bring it over to the right.

19. Reverse-fold the middle layer of paper as far as it will go.

20. Enlarged view. Reverse-fold the edge as far as it will go. Repeat behind.

21. Mountain-fold the corners into the belly.

22. Valley-fold the layers in the belly as shown. Repeat behind.

23. Mountain-fold the front of the legs underneath.

24. Double-reverse-fold the tails of the coat. Reverse-fold the top of the head. Mountain-fold the belly. Reverse-fold the feet upwards. Repeat behind.

25. Enlarged view of head. Reverse-fold the hair down.

26. Like so.

27. Enlarged view of foot. Reverse-fold the top of the foot down. Reverse-fold the tip and the bottom inside. Repeat on the other foot.

28. Completed foot.

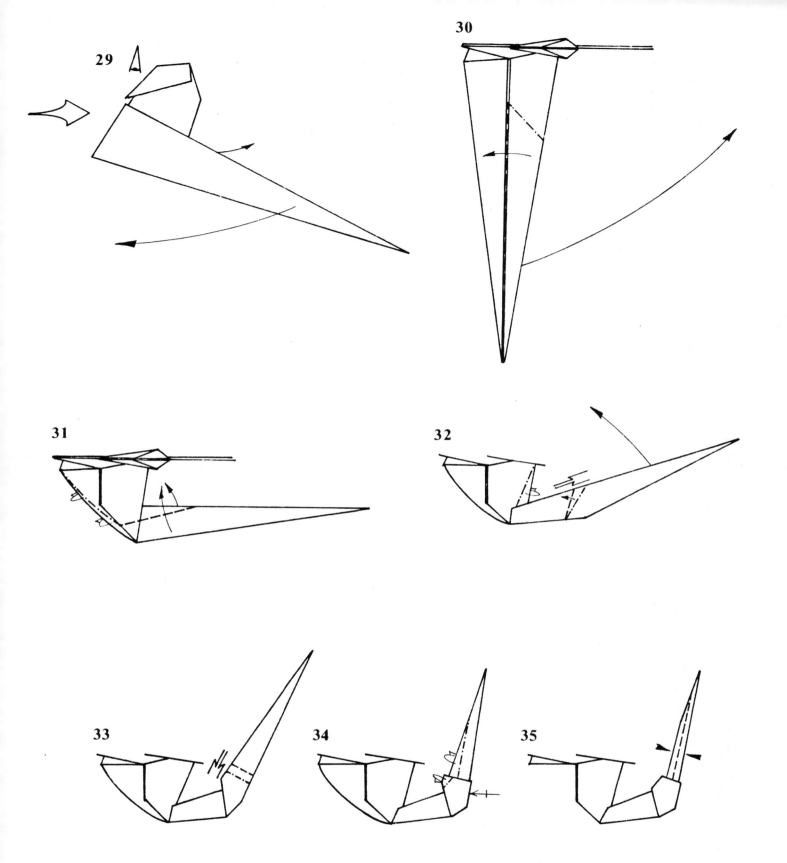

29. Pull the right arm out away from the body.

30. View from 29. Reverse-fold the arm forward, wrapping the inside layer over the outside layer.

31. Outside-reverse-fold the forearm.

32. Mountain-fold the edge of the arm. Crimp the hand.

33. Crimp the hand again to form a bow.

34. Mountain-fold the hand and bow. Repeat below.

35. Pinch the bow.

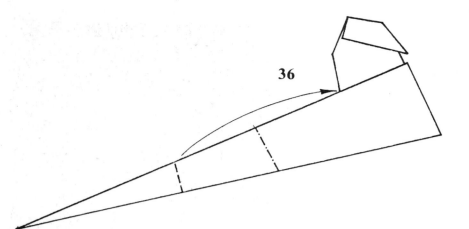

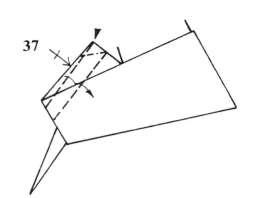

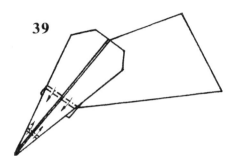

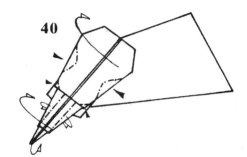

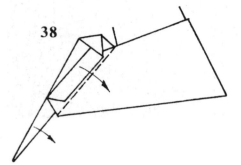

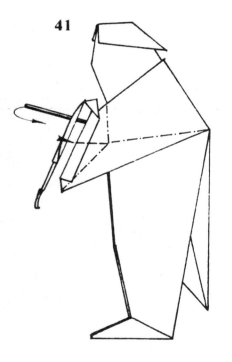

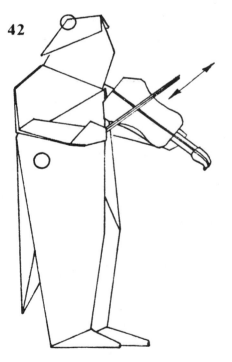

36. Reverse-fold the right arm.
37. Squash-fold and valley-fold the edges down. Repeat behind.
38. Open the violin out flat.
39. Crimp the head and neck of the violin.
40. Shape the neck and body with mountain folds. Push in

the sides, and curl the head around behind. Pivot the violin around so it lies under the chin of the violinist.
41. Sink the inside of the elbow so the arm comes up to support the violin. Turn the model over.
42. Finished Violinist. Hold at the circles and pull. The Violinist will play the violin.

Bassist

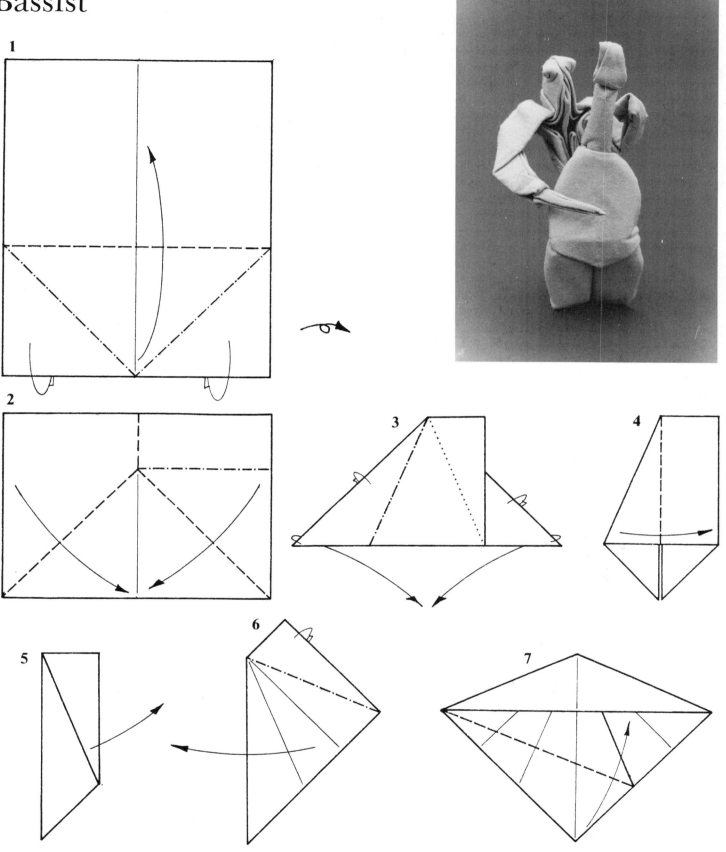

Paper: Use a 1:1.207 rectangle, colored side up.

1. Mountain-fold the lower corners underneath and fold the resulting point upward. Turn the model over from side to side.

2. Rabbit-ear the remaining paper.

3. Mountain-fold the edges behind.

4. Fold the left side over to the right.

5. Pull out the trapped layers of paper.

6. Swing one layer from the right over to the left and squash down the top of the model.

7. Valley-fold an edge upward.

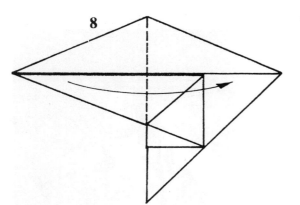

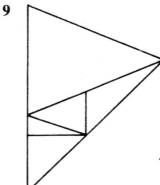

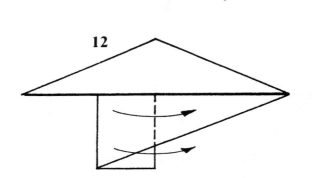

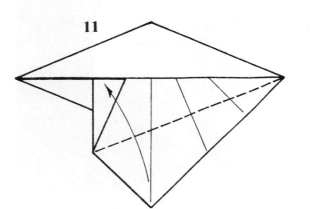

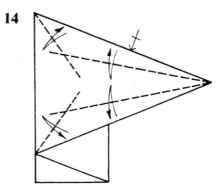

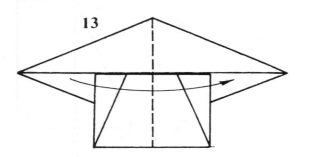

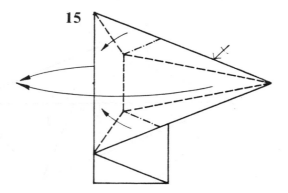

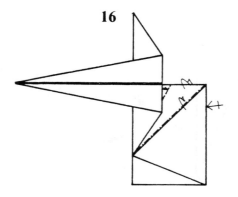

8. Fold the left point over to the right.
9. Turn the model over from side to side.
10. Fold the top layer over to the right.
11. Fold the bottom edge upward.
12. Fold one layer over to the right (the layer extends up under the "hood" at the top of the model).

13. Fold the entire model in half.
14. Enlarged view. Crease the angle bisectors.
15. Double-rabbit-ear both sides.
16. Pull out as much as possible from the right of the body and tuck the excess under the triangle at the far right. Repeat behind.

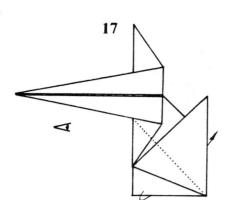

17

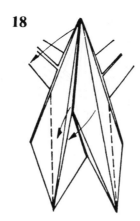

18

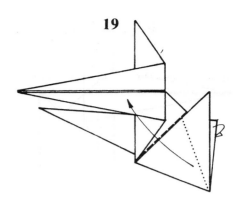

19

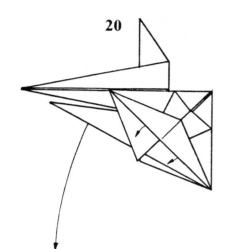

20

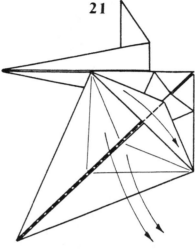

21

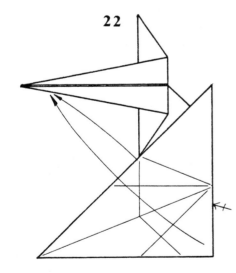

22

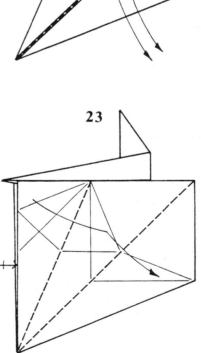

23

17. Reverse-fold the middle layer of paper.

18. View from 17. Reverse-fold outward the large flap trapped in the middle layers of the paper.

19. Fold one layer from the bottom upward and squash the region of the paper exposed at the right.

20. Pull the long triangle downward and open it. In the process, you will release several layers of paper trapped under the little hood.

21. Fold the long point in half and pull the loose flaps out from the interior.

22. Fold the large flaps up as far as possible, in front and behind.

23. Fold over and over, front and behind.

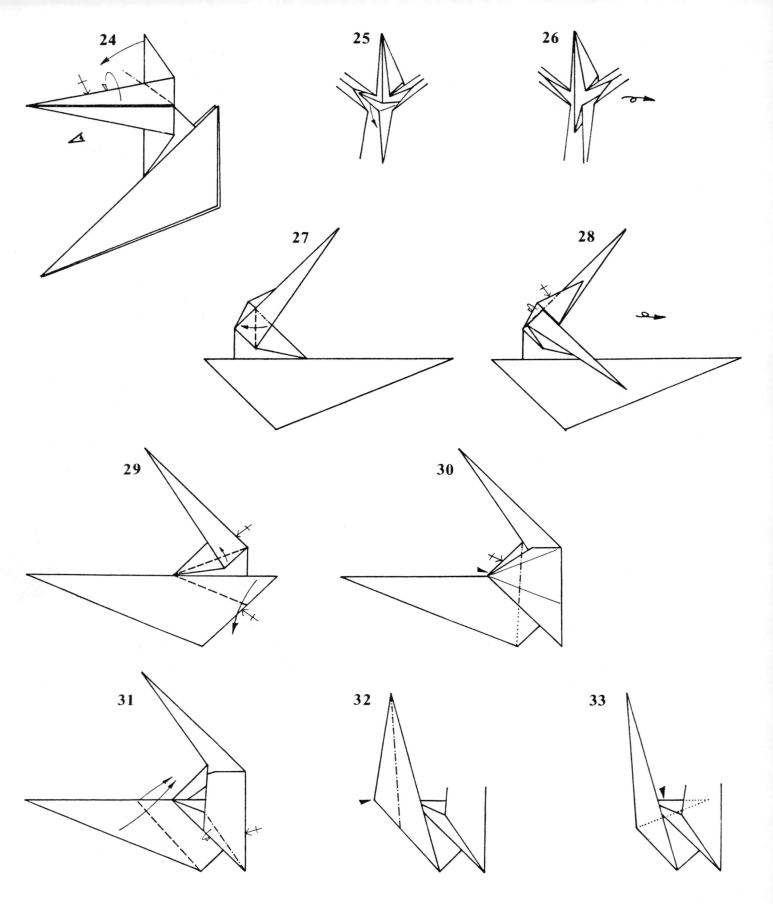

24. Crimp the head (the top point) downward. Three layers go one way, two go the other.

25. View from 24. Fold the middle layer pleat downward.

26. Like this. Close the model up and turn it over.

27. Pivot the arm.

28. Mountain-fold the edges of the head. Turn the paper over.

29. Valley-fold the skinny triangle under the arm. Repeat behind. Valley-fold the foot (at the right) downward. Repeat behind.

30. Closed-sink the indicated point. Repeat behind.

31. Reverse-fold the point at the left (the bass). Mountain-fold the edge of the leg. Repeat behind.

32. Sink the long edge.

33. Sink the indicated region.

34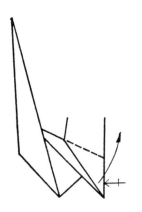

35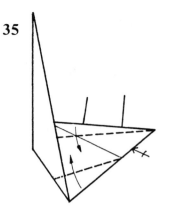

36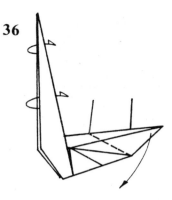

37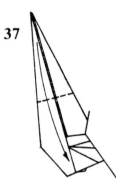

38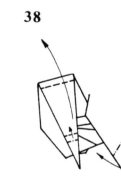

39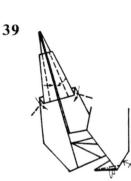

40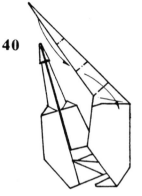

41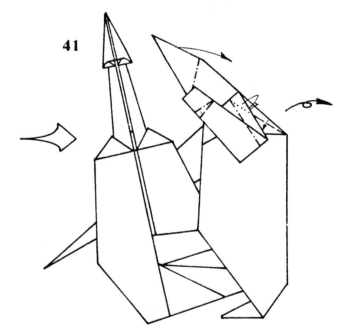

42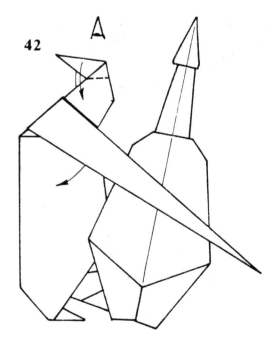

34. Valley-fold the leg upwards.

35. Valley-fold the top. Reverse-fold the bottom. Repeat behind.

36. Fold the legs back down. Swing the bass open.

37. Fold the top half of the bass downward.

38. Pleat the neck and head of the bass. Reverse-fold the feet.

39. Narrow the neck of the bass and the feet.

40. Reverse-fold the tip of the left arm. Pleat it to make an elbow.

41. Enlarged view. Mountain-fold the edge of the arm to lock the shoulder and elbow. Crimp the hand. Reverse-fold the head.

42. Reverse-fold the hair. Open the right arm out away from the body.

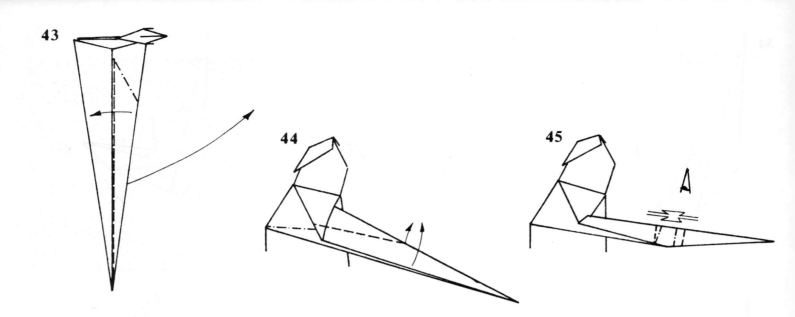

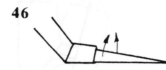

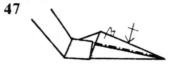

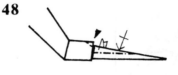

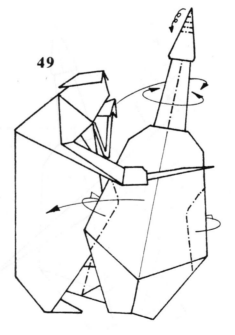

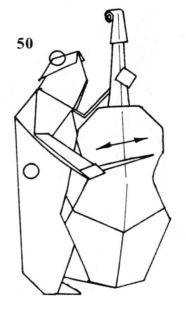

43. View from 42. Reverse-fold the arm to point forward.

44. Outside-reverse-fold the arm.

45. Crimp the hand and a bow.

46. View from 45 of hand. Pull the extra layers of paper off of the bow.

47. Mountain-fold the layers inside.

48. Narrow the bow and round the hand.

49. Shape the body of the bass with mountain folds. Pleat the base of the model and twist the bass so that it stands out away from the body. Curl the top of the bass.

50. Finished Bassist. Hold the head and body of the Bassist and pull. He will bow his bass.

Pianist

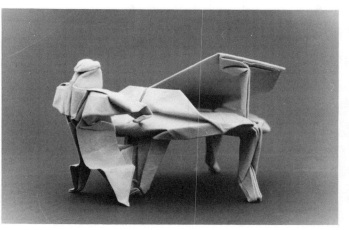

1

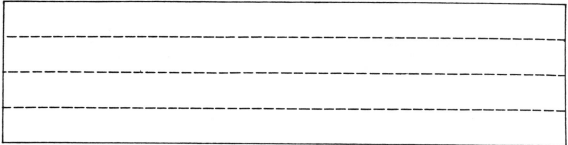

2

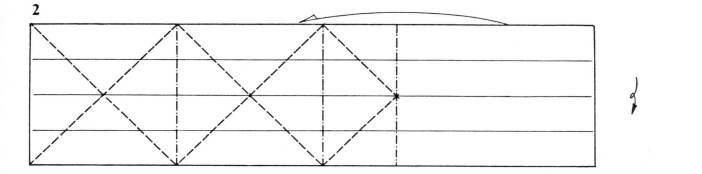

3

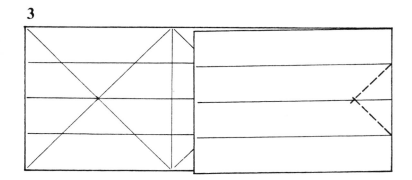

4

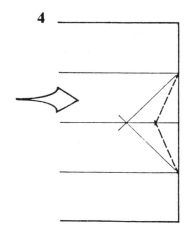

Paper: Use a 1:3.874 rectangle of thin paper or foil-backed paper, colored side up. It is also possible to start with a 1:4 rectangle and cut off the excess after step 8.

1. Divide the paper into fourths with horizontal creases.

2. Crease 2½ squares, starting from the left, using diagonal valley folds. Delineate them with vertical mountain folds.

Leave the last mountain fold in place and turn the paper over.

3. Crease the small triangle through both layers of paper with angle bisectors.

4. Enlarged view. Bisect the angle again.

133

5

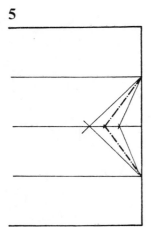

6

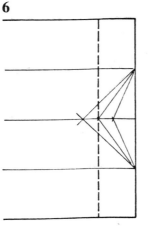

7

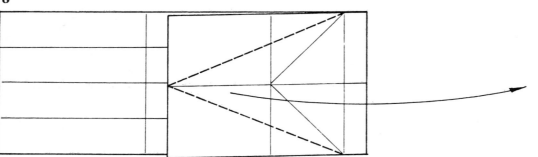

8

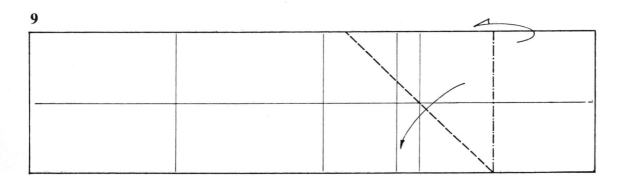

9

10

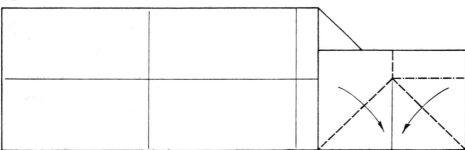

5. Bisect the new angles with mountain folds, again through both layers of paper.

6. Put a valley fold through the intersection shown.

7. Crease half of a square with the valley folds shown. The right ends of the folds terminate at the crease made in step 6.

8. Bisect the angles made by the creases of step 7 and the edges. The two creases should meet in the middle of the end of the paper, if you have made all the preceding creases precise. If you started with a longer rectangle, now is the time to cut off any excess that extends beyond the intersection of these two creases. Unfold the right side.

9. The mountain fold lies on an existing crease. Fold it down to lie along the bottom edge of the paper.

10. Rabbit-ear the flap on the right.

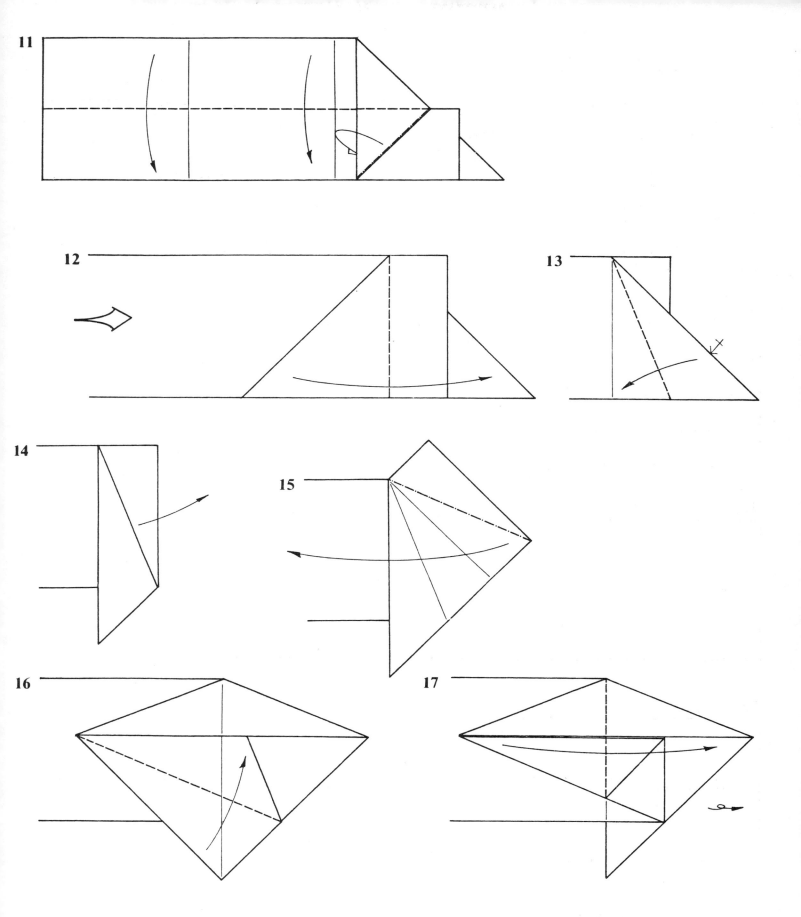

11. Valley-fold the top of the flap downward and reverse-fold its right side.

12. Enlarged view. Fold the triangular flap over to the right.

13. Valley-fold the right edge down to lie along the vertical crease.

14. Pull out the trapped layers of paper.

15. Fold the top layer all the way over to the left. The upper corner will open out and move down.

16. Valley-fold one layer.

17. Book-fold the point from the left over to the right. Turn the paper over from side to side.

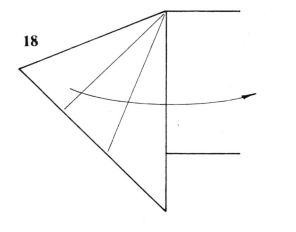

18

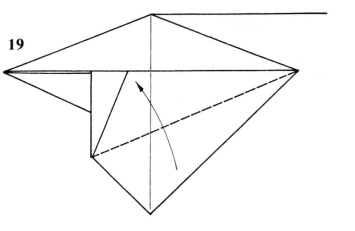

19

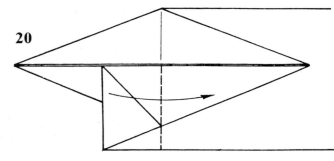

20

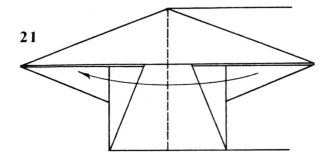

21

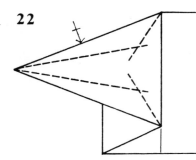

22

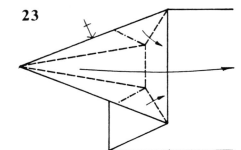

23

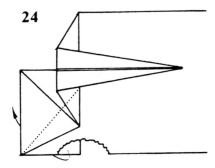

24

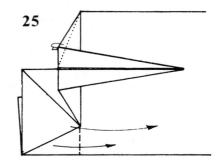

25

26

18. Book-fold one layer as far as possible.
19. Valley-fold.
20. Book-fold one layer.
21. Book-fold both layers together as one.
22. Crease the angle bisectors. Repeat behind.
23. Double-rabbit-ear. Repeat behind.

24. Reverse-fold the hidden corner.
25. Bring one layer over to the right and swing the arms (the long, skinny points) outward.
26. Valley-fold the arms and mountain-fold the edges of the body in to lie along the center line.

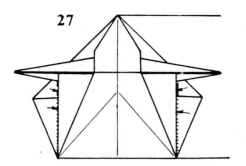

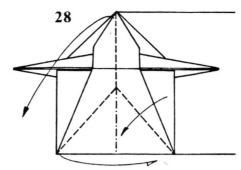

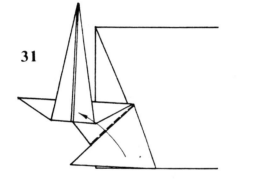

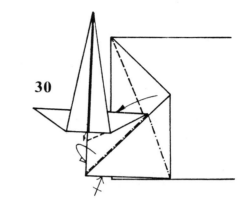

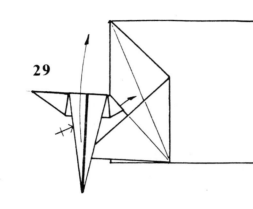

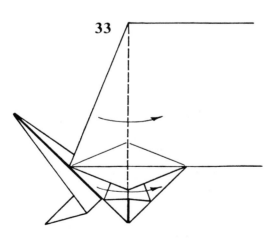

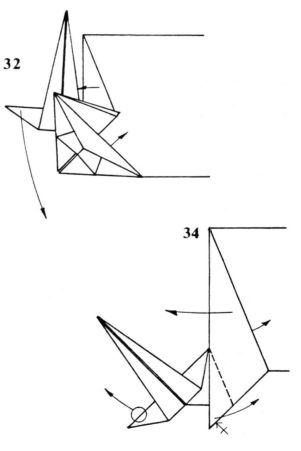

27. Reverse-fold the sides.

28. Rabbit-ear the body. Swing the left side behind.

29. Swing the arms back up and pull out the layers of paper trapped at the right.

30. Pull the excess paper out of the back and tuck it behind the triangles at the bottom left corner. Repeat behind. Reverse-fold the edges on the right side of the body.

31. Swing one layer upwards and squash-fold.

32. Swing the body down and release the layers trapped under the hood at the bottom of the model.

33. Fold the body in half.

34. Pull the extra paper out of the body. Valley-fold the small triangles down.

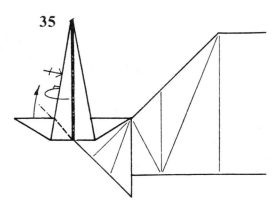

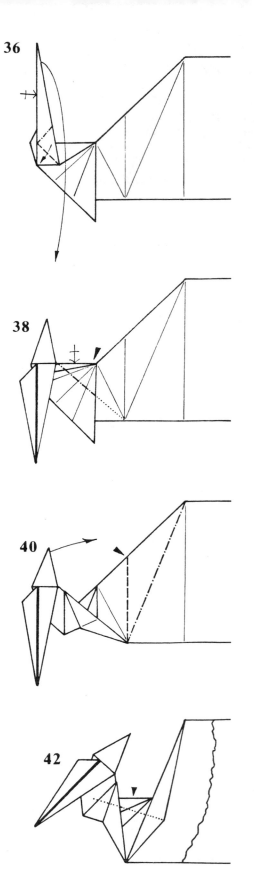

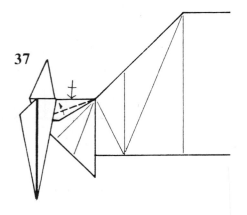

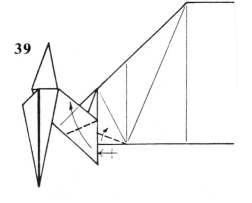

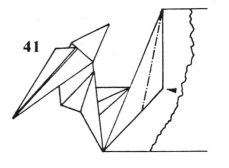

35. Crimp the head forward.
36. Squash-fold the arms.
37. Valley-fold the indicated edge upward. Repeat behind.
38. Closed-sink the triangular region. Repeat behind.
39. Swivel-fold the leg upwards.

40. Crimp the body of the man to the right. Both creases already exist.
41. Sink the long edge inside the model.
42. Sink the triangular region.

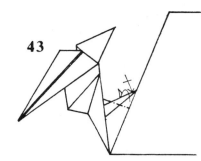

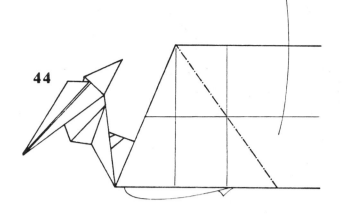

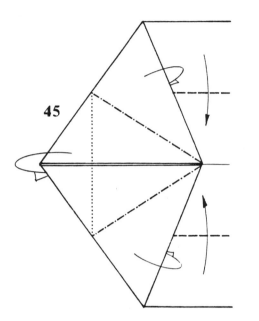

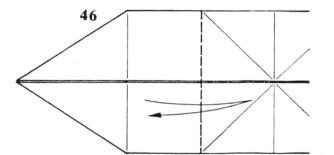

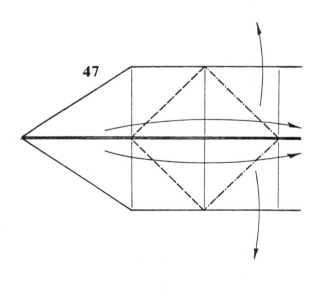

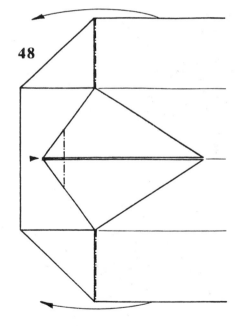

43. Mountain-fold the triangular flaps downward.

44. Open out the rest of the paper and pivot the pianist counterclockwise.

45. In this and following drawings, the piano player has been omitted since he would cover up relevant folds. Petal fold the flap that contains the pianist.

46. Crease a valley fold at the location shown.

47. Open out the sides of the long part of the paper and swing the pianist back over to the right.

48. Closed-sink about one-third of the blunt point. Mountain-fold the rest of the paper behind.

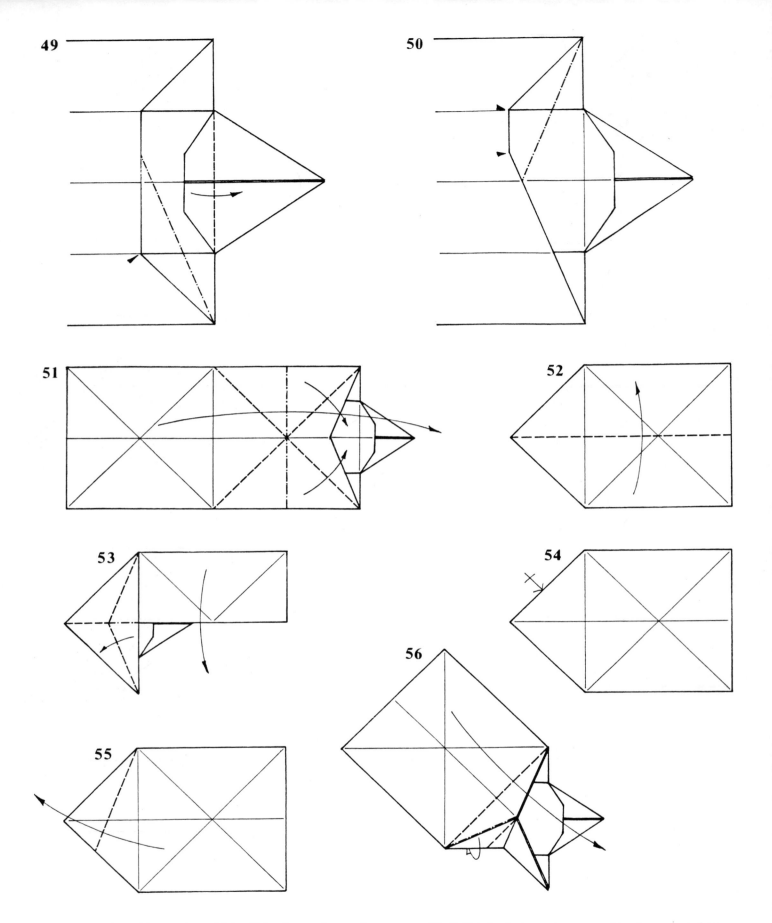

49. Fold the blunt point (which will be the music stand) to the right. Closed-sink the corner indicated.

50. Closed-sink the other corner.

51. Reduced view. Fold a Waterbomb Base with the square region shown.

52. Fold the bottom upwards.

53. Fold it back down, incorporating the creases shown.

54. Repeat steps 52 and 53 on the top.

55. Valley-fold along the angle bisector.

56. Mountain-fold the lower edge behind. Fold the large square down to the right.

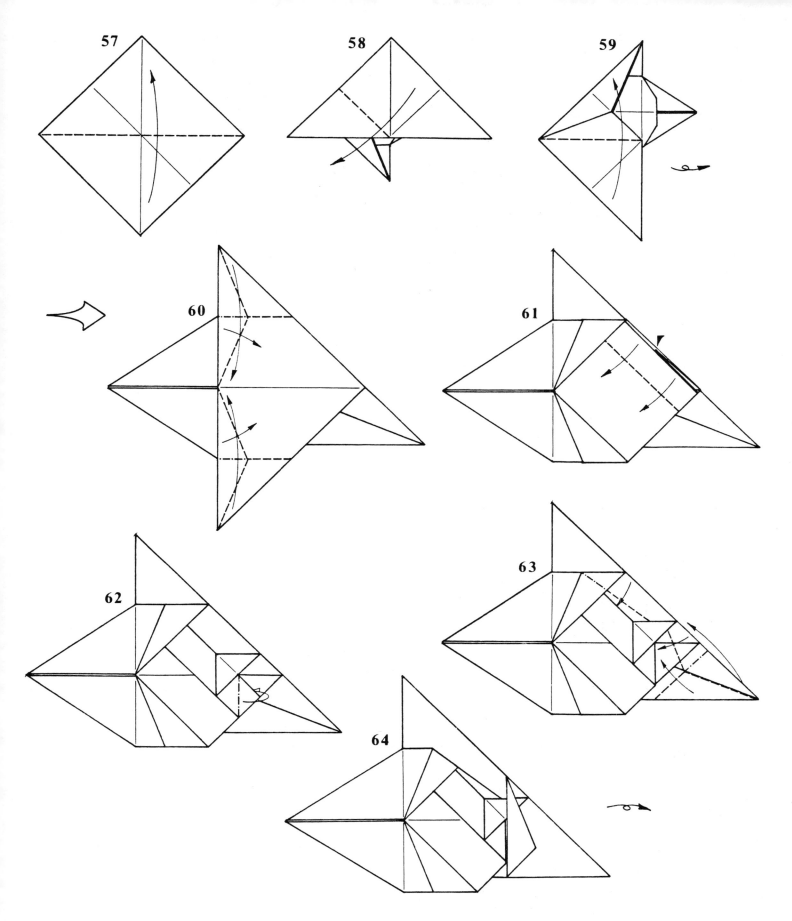

57. Fold the square in half along the diagonal.
58. Fold the flap down to the left.
59. Fold the triangular flap upwards. Turn the model over.
60. Enlarged view. Rabbit-ear two flaps.
61. Valley-fold the layer shown. Squash-fold the corner underneath.

62. Mountain-fold the small triangle.
63. Reverse-fold the edge at the top. Rabbit-ear the right point.
64. Turn the model over.

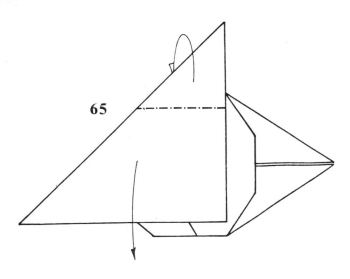

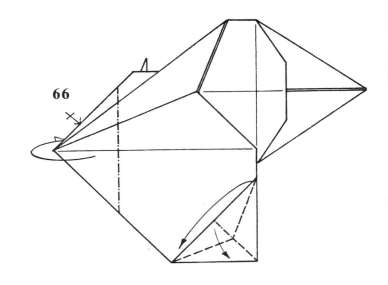

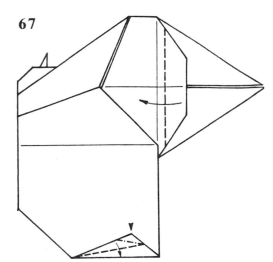

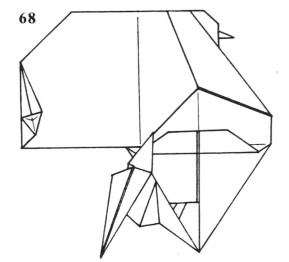

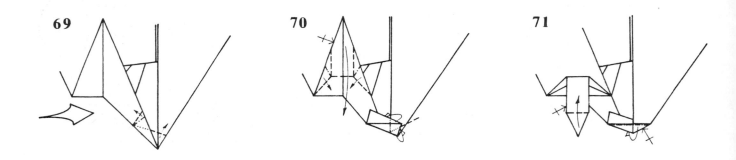

65. Mountain-fold the tip of the triangle underneath so that the same amount of piano shows at the the top as at the bottom. Fold the entire flap down.

66. Mountain-fold the left corner inside the model. Repeat with the layer below it. Rabbit-ear the point on the corner.

67. Fold the music stand up. Spread-sink the corner at the bottom.

68. The result, showing the pianist.

69. Enlarged view of the pianist's feet. Crimp and swivel the foot.

70. Double-rabbit-ear the legs of the bench. Reverse-fold the tip of the foot. Repeat behind.

71. Valley-fold the bench leg. Mountain-fold the bottom of the foot. Repeat behind.

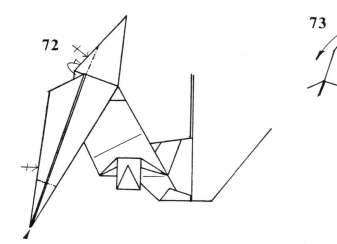

72

73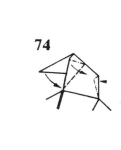

74

75

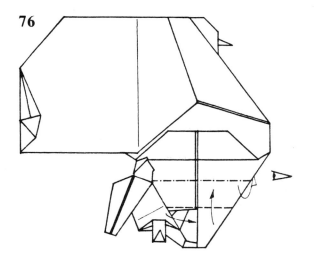

76

77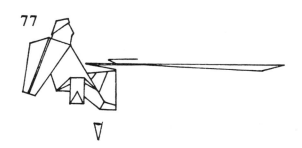

78

79

72. Sink the tips of the arms. Mountain-fold the edges of the back of the head.
73. Detail of head. Reverse-fold the head.
74. Outside-reverse-fold the hair. Dent under the nose.
75. Finished head.
76. Pleat the keyboard; swing the pianist out away from the piano and swing the rest of the piano down.

77. View from 76. Like this.
78. View from 77. Swivel-fold the edges of the keyboard. Reverse-fold the three legs.
79. Reverse-fold the feet of the piano.

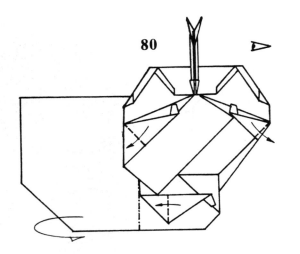

80

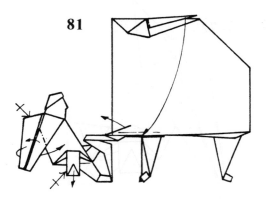

81

82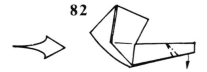

83

84

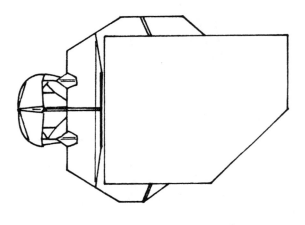

80. Swing the legs out away from the piano body and fold the top behind.

81. View from 80. Reverse-fold the arms forward. Fold the legs of the bench down. Lift up the music stand. Fold the top support down and tuck its tip under a flap at the edge of the piano.

82. Enlarged view of arm. Squash the hand out flat.

83. Like this.

84. Finished Pianist. Hold his head and back and pull, and he will move his hands across the keyboard.

Cuckoo Clock

1

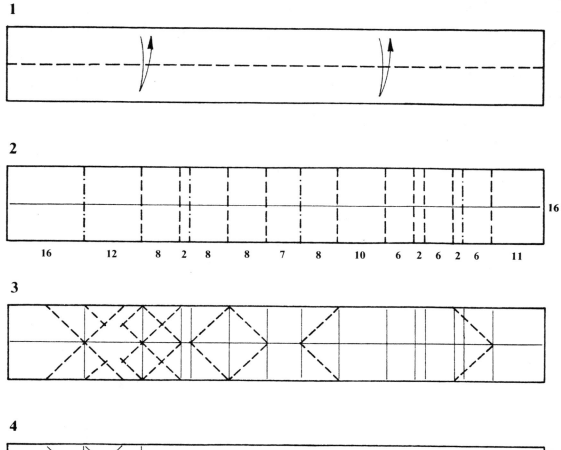

2

16

16   12   8   2   8   8   7   8   10   6   2   6   2   6   11

3

4

5

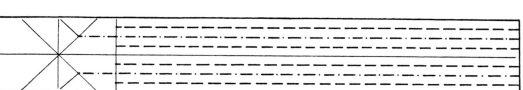

Paper: Use a 1:7 rectangle of foil-backed paper, white side up.

1. Fold the paper in half horizontally and unfold.

2. Measure the short dimension of the paper and divide that amount by 16. That becomes one unit. Make the vertical creases, spacing them according to the number of units indicated along the bottom. These creases are used as reference points throughout the model, so be accurate.

3. Make the diagonal creases shown.

4. Add the horizontal creases.

5. Fold a Waterbomb Base at the left side.

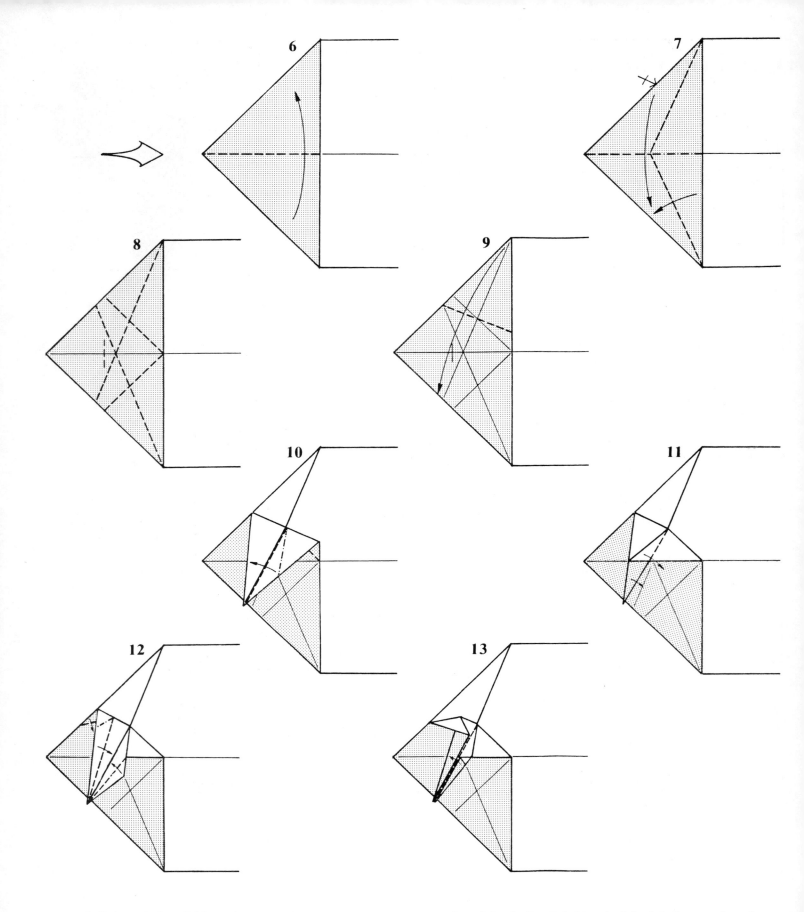

6. Enlarged view. Fold one layer up.

7. Fold the layer back down, incorporating the reverse fold. Repeat steps 6 and 7 on the upper flap.

8. Crease the angle bisectors and locate the point halfway between the left tip and the right edge.

9. Fold the point down to the left. The valley fold runs through the intersection of the two angle bisectors creased in

step 8, and the tip lies slightly to the left of the intersection of crease and edge.

10. Swivel-fold.

11. Fold the flap back to the right.

12. Narrow the flap with a valley fold and a swivel fold.

13. Fold the point in half.

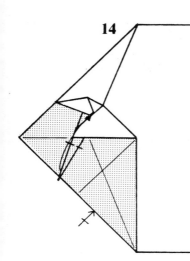 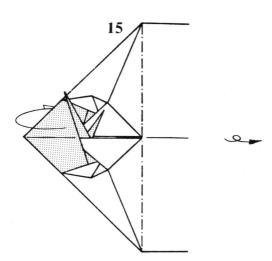 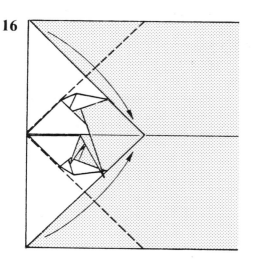

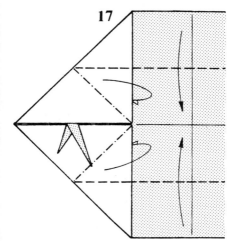 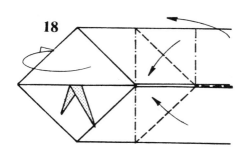 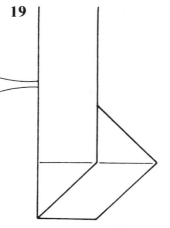

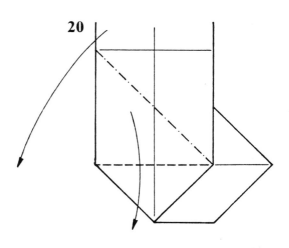 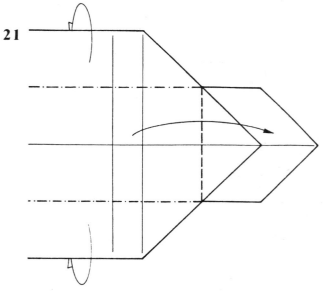

14. Fold the tip back to the upper right. Repeat steps 9–13 on the lower flap.

15. Mountain-fold the triangle behind, and turn the model over from top to bottom.

16. Valley-fold the corners in to the center. Bring the two points (hands of the clock face) out through the slit.

17. Reverse-fold the sides.

18. Rabbit-ear the long part of the model. Mountain-fold the left side behind.

19. Pull out the hidden layers of paper.

20. Squash-fold the long part of the model.

21. Petal-fold the long part of the model.

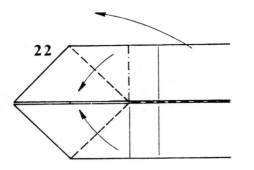

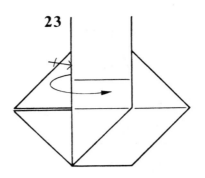

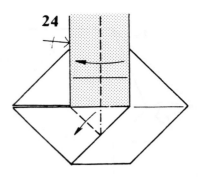

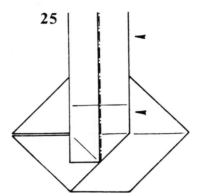

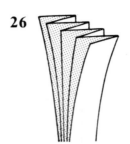

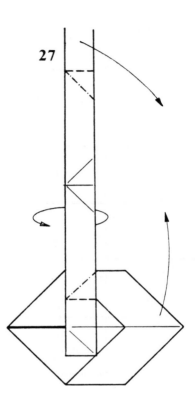

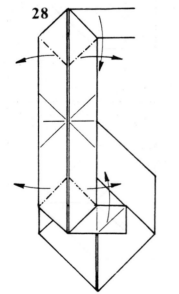

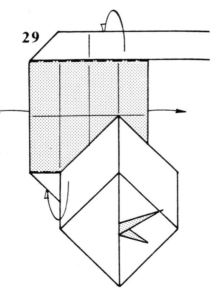

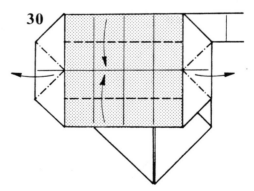

22. Form another rabbit ear with the long part.

23. Pull the hidden layers out and wrap them around the outside. Repeat behind.

24. Valley-fold the long edge. Pull out the triangular region at the bottom. Repeat behind.

25. Sink the long edge.

26. The result should be pleated all the way to the end, like this.

27. Open the section of the long pleat shown. The top and bottom get squash-folded, so that the face of the clock and the rest of the paper pivot. The valley folds are on existing creases. (The sequence of steps 27–30 make two successive Elias stretches).

28. Open the raw edges and pivot the clock face and the rest of the model closer together.

29. Do the same thing on the opposite side.

30. Pull the ends apart, and pivot the face and the rest of the model closer together.

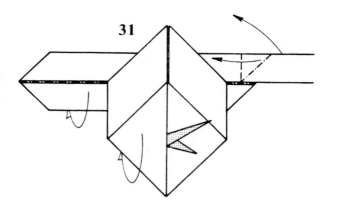

31

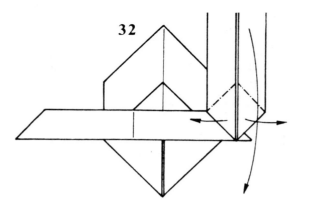

32

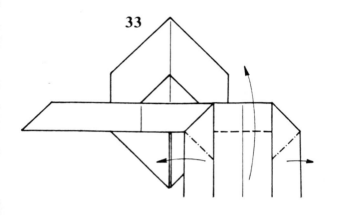

33

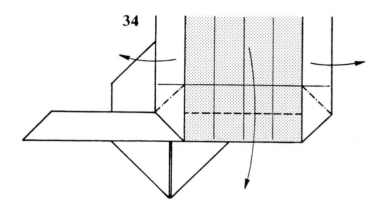

34

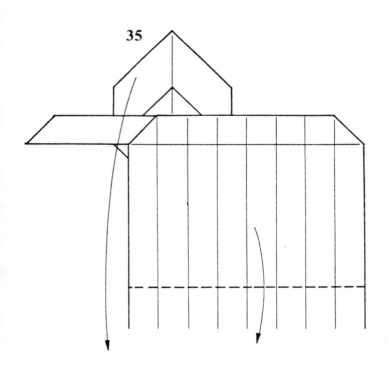

35

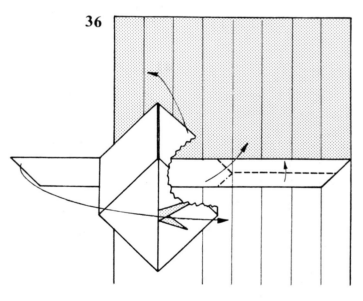

36

31. Squash-fold the remaining paper. The valley fold is on an existing crease. Mountain-fold the clock face behind.

32. Open the edges and fold down the remainder of the paper (another Elias stretch in progress).

33. Repeat step 32, folding the paper back up.

34. Again, back down. Elias stretch complete.

35. Valley-fold the assembly down on an existing crease.

36. Swing the section of paper connecting the face and back upward so that it is vertical and centered on the back. It will be necessary to form the horizontal valley fold shown. The leftmost point pivots down.

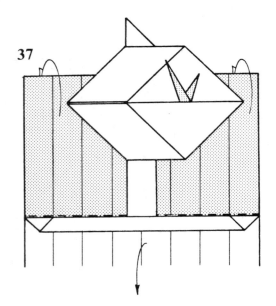

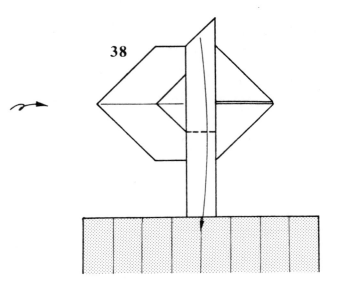

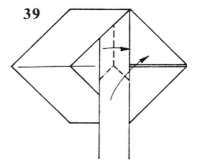

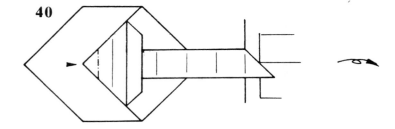

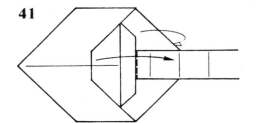

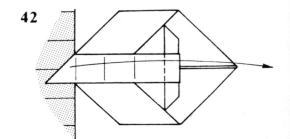

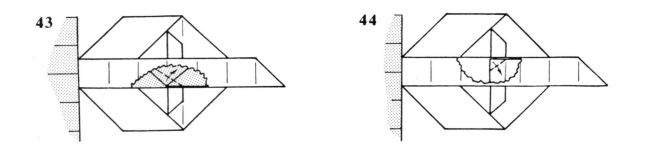

37. Pull the face of the clock upwards (there is a flap extending down from the face that is not shown here). Turn the model over from side to side.

38. Fold one flap down as far as it will go.

39. Fold everything over to the right, forming the vertical valley fold exactly as was done in step 36.

40. Sink the corner shown.

41. Pivot the face around the flap sticking out to the right. Turn the model over from side to side.

42. Fold the point shown over to the right.

43. Locate the hidden layer and fold it over as far as it will go.

44. Do the same on the other side. These two locking folds are critical to the action mechanism.

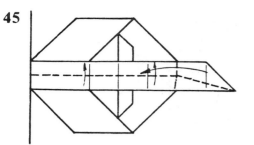

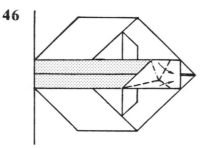

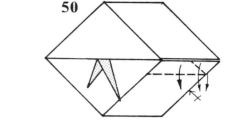

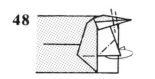

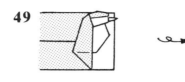

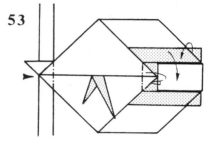

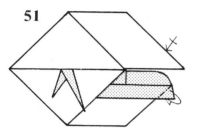

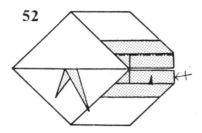

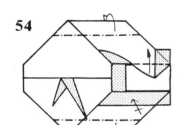

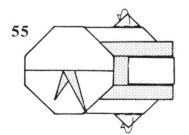

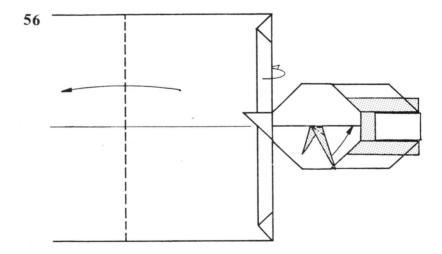

45. Fold the right tip back to the left. Simultaneously, make the long valley fold.

46. Form an asymmetric rabbit ear.

47. Detail of cuckoo. Crimp the head downward.

48. Crimp the beak. Reverse-fold the layers of the belly inward.

49. Like so. Turn the model over.

50. Detail of clock face. Valley-fold the front and back layers. The tip is opened out and wrapped around. This is rather difficult to perform.

51. The wrap is almost completed. Flatten the paper out and repeat on the upper layer.

52. Sink the long edges.

53. Mountain-fold the right corner of the clock face behind. Sink the left corner. Pull the hidden layer out from the right.

54. Mountain-fold the top and bottom edges behind. Close up the flap pulled out in step 53. Repeat on the lower portion of the clock face.

55. Mountain-fold the corners.

56. Valley-fold on an existing crease, but keep the clock face in the same orientation. Squash-fold the big hand.

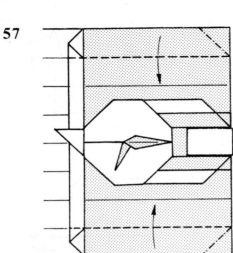

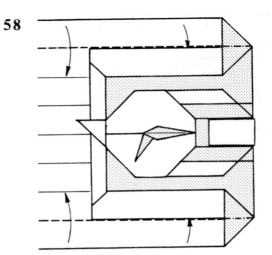

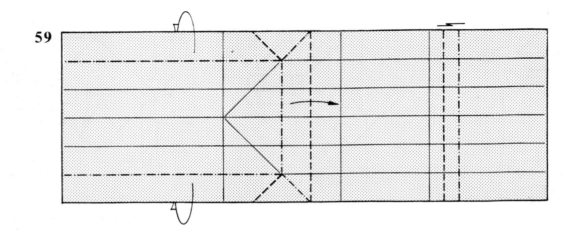

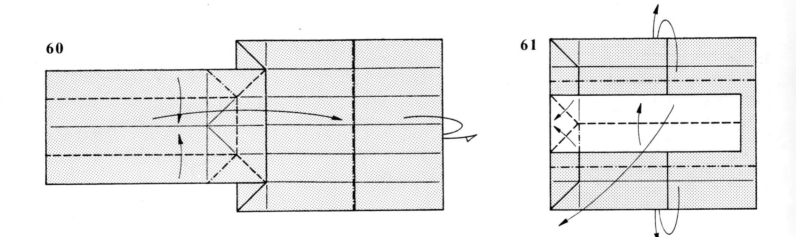

57. Squash-fold a single layer at the top and bottom.

58. Tuck the edges underneath. Turn the model over from top to bottom.

59. Pleat the top layer of paper at the right. The vertical mountain fold lies on an existing crease, and the valley fold lies between it and the next crease. Fold in the edges of the remainder with the vertical pleat on the left.

60. Crease a mountain fold through two layers at the base of the pleat on the right. Double-rabbit-ear the long flap on the left.

61. Crease the mountain folds by bringing the edges in to the center. Rabbit-ear the long flap.

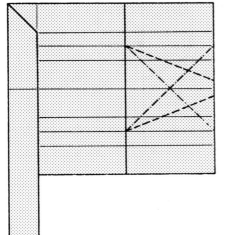

62

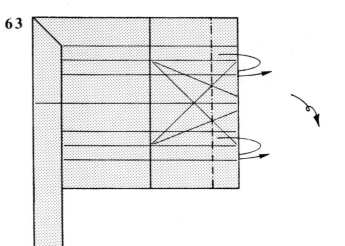

63

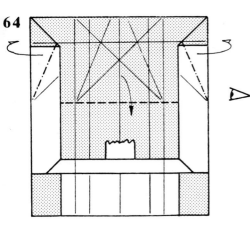

64

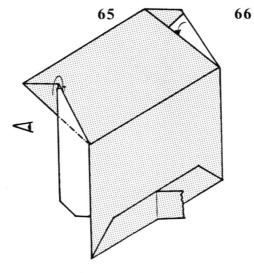

65

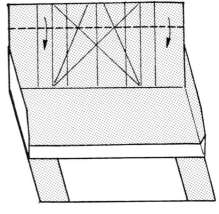

66

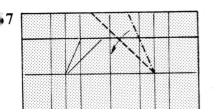

7

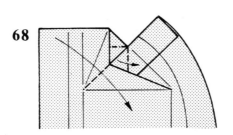

68

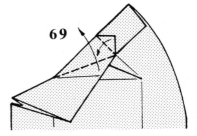

69

62. Crease the angle bisectors.

63. Crease the mountain fold that runs through the angle bisectors' intersection. Turn the model over from side to side and rotate clockwise 90 degrees.

64. Valley-fold the roof down at 135 degrees and wrap the sides upwards.

65. View from 64. Tuck the vertical flaps under the edges of the roof.

66. View from 65. Valley-fold the top edge down on the crease made in step 63.

67. Detail of top edge of roof. Pleat the right on existing creases. The paper will not lie flat.

68. Fold the left side down, pulling the small central region out to the right.

69. Fold the little triangle over to the left. Then, cover it up by folding the left side upwards.

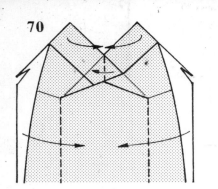

70

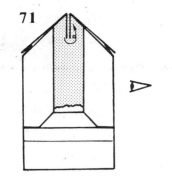

71

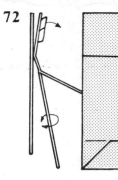

72

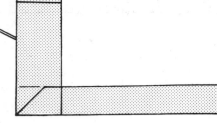

73

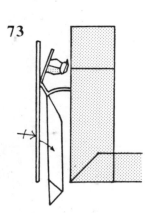

74

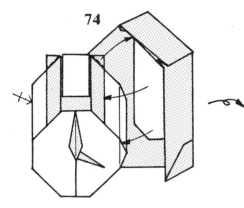

75

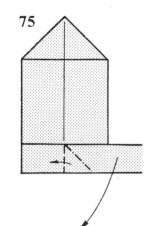

76

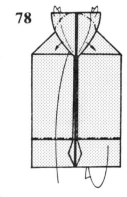

77

78

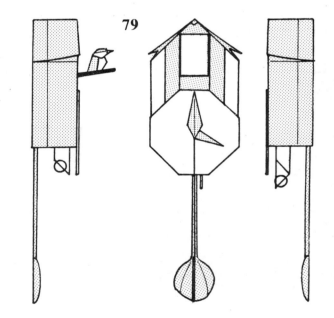

79

70. Bring the two halves of the roof together and pull out the corners folded in step 66 so that they point straight down.

71. Roll the two corners together so that they lock the roof together.

72. View from 71. This shows the clock face, the cuckoo, the lever, and the paper connecting them all to the body of the clock. Pull down the bird at right angles to the trap door, and mountain-fold the lever in half (you will have to make it a rabbit ear at the upper end).

73. Pull the sides of the clock face out at right angles to the rest of the face.

74. Assemble the clock. The sides of the body go under the face and the narrow flaps extending up from it, while the

corners of the face get tucked into the edge of the roof. Turn the clock over.

75. Squash-fold the long flap poking out from the back.

76. Petal-fold the flap.

77. Pleat the length of the long flap to narrow it, but pull out the layers of paper at the upper end.

78. Mountain-fold the edges of the pendulum to round it. Reverse-fold the bottom of the clock up inside. The pendulum swings down. This completes locking the clock together.

79. Finished Cuckoo Clock. Hold the lever where indicated, and push up to make the cuckoo pop out.